Leonard Woolsey Bacon

Irenics and Polemics

With Sundry Essays in Church History

Leonard Woolsey Bacon

Irenics and Polemics
With Sundry Essays in Church History

ISBN/EAN: 9783744754347

Printed in Europe, USA, Canada, Australia, Japan

Cover: Foto ©Lupo / pixelio.de

More available books at **www.hansebooks.com**

IRENICS AND POLEMICS

WITH SUNDRY

ESSAYS IN CHURCH HISTORY

BY

LEONARD WOOLSEY BACON

———

NEW YORK:
THE CHRISTIAN LITERATURE CO.
1895

COPYRIGHT, 1895, BY
THE CHRISTIAN LITERATURE CO.

CONTENTS

⁂ The several papers comprised in this volume stand in the order in which they were published or republished, in the "CHRISTIAN LITERATURE" Magazine. In the following table, the titles are disposed in a more logical order

IRENICS AND POLEMICS

	PAGE
THE AMERICAN CHURCH AND THE PRIMITIVE CHURCH	225
FIVE THEORIES OF THE CHURCH	230
THE RESTORATION OF THE PROTESTANT EPISCOPAL CHURCH TO CATHOLIC FELLOWSHIP	273
HOW THE REVEREND DOCTOR STONE BETTERED HIS SITUATION	57

ESSAYS IN CHURCH HISTORY

THE REAL PRISONER OF CHILLON (1400-1570)	109
CONCERNING THE USE OF FAGOTS AT GENEVA (1553)	205
TWO SIDES TO A SAINT (1567-1622)	1
WILLIAM LLOYD GARRISON (1805-1870)	145

TWO SIDES TO A SAINT

This historical essay, written at Geneva, was published in *Macmillan's Magazine*, London, for September, 1878, and has since been reissued as a pamphlet at Lausanne, Switzerland, with the consent both of author and of publishers.

On its first appearance, it was the subject of very serious attention in England and America, from critics of very different schools. The London *Academy* declared it to be " one of the most telling and vigorous pieces of historical criticism that we have met with for a long time," and concluded, " in a word, this article is one which the apologists of St. Francis and his 'sweetness' will do well to answer. If they pass it by, the world may well be excused for believing that it is unanswerable." In like manner, the London *Church Times*, from the opposite point of view, representing the party that has been devoted to the cult of St. Francis, recognized the seriousness of the issue, and came to the same conclusion, " unless Mr. Bacon's article is answered, *we shall have to give up St. Francis de Sales.*"

Well, more than sixteen years have passed, and the article is still "unanswered because unanswerable;" but we are still waiting for indications that this prostrate and discredited idol, so

" Lopp'd, maim'd and battered on the grundsel edge,"

is any the less an object of veneration to its English votaries.

TWO SIDES TO A SAINT.*

THE titles given below are far from representing all that has lately been published in England on the subject of St. Francis de Sales. The amount and character of this literature indicate a degree of reverent interest in that remarkable man almost amounting to a new *cultus*. The feeling is manifested, not only by the authors of these books (in whom something is to be pardoned to the enthusiasm of biography), but also by the readers and critics, that in the person of "the Apostle of the Chablais," we have a type of sanctified humanity quite superior to anything that can be expected from the English stock, and which mere Protestantism cannot attain unto. Now

---

* *St. Francis de Sales, Bishop and Prince of Geneva.* By the author of *A Dominican Artist*. Rivingtons, 1876.
A Selection from the Spiritual Letters of St. Francis de Sales. Translated by the same author. Rivingtons, 1871.
The Spirit of St. Francis de Sales. By Jean Pierre Camus, Bishop of Belley. Translated by the same author. Rivingtons, 1872.
The Mission of St. Francis of Sales in the Chablais. By Lady Herbert. Bentley, 1868.
Selections from the Letters of St. Francis de Sales. Translated from the French by Mrs. C. W. Bagot. Revised by a Priest of the English Church. Masters, 1871.
The "Salesian" literature in French, always voluminous, has received unusual increments of late, in consequence of the project just accomplished, for constituting St. Francis a "doctor of the Church."

there is nothing but good to be said of the naturalization of foreign saints, provided only it be done with discretion and fidelity to historic truth. But there is large scope here for the function of the *avvocato del diavolo;* and we are bound to say of all these books that they are wholly negligent of this duty. The Francis de Sales whom they present to us is neither the legendary Francis nor the historical Francis. The blaze of color which characterizes the legend is toned down to suit the English taste, though no attempt is made to correct the drawing. Not even Lady Herbert's *Mission in the Chablais* ventures to reproduce that wild profusion of miracle, and those unctuous details concerning the saint's resistance to temptation, in which his panegyrists so much delight. Not even the author of *A Dominican Artist*, in whose writings appear so many indications of industry and good taste, ventures on anything, with regard to the facts of her hero's life, but a servile though distant and timid following of the Roman Catholic tradition.

It is not necessary to go beyond Francis's own letters and the documents of his friends and partisans for the materials for correcting these distorted representations; and it is not creditable to intelligent writers who have had these materials under their eyes, to persist in repeating the old fiction as truth. A less labor-saving course would not only be more honorable to themselves, and more just to their readers, but it would not be in all respects disadvantageous to their hero. He would doubtless lose some rays of the halo that envelops him; he might be constrained to descend a step or two from that lofty pedestal on which he seems sometimes to be consciously posing for a saint; and certainly there would be some qualifying of that preternatural sweetness which (to the Protestant taste) approaches now and then the very verge of mawkishness; but whatever his portrait might lose in heroic dimensions and in the air of sanctity, not to say sanctimony, it would gain in human interest and probability. In the early pages of his biography, we should miss that solemn little prig described in the bull of canonization as having "shown when a child none of the traits of childhood," and in the eulogy of Father Morel as "having manifested in the cradle such chaste modesty as to shrink from the caresses of his nurse, and hardly permit her to kiss him;"* and in the later chapters we

---

* *Canonisation de St. François de Sales, en 16 discours.* Grenoble, 1665.

should part with more regret from the figure of "the Apostle of the Chablais," taking his life in his hand and encountering the lofty mountains of the Chablais, its frightful precipices, its eternal winters, its ferocious beasts and still more savage inhabitants, opposing the malignity and heresy of the latter only with the arms of love and meekness, and with the eloquent preaching of the true faith, until "at last his gentleness triumphed over their brutality, his love over their hate, his patience over their fury, his constancy to serve them over their obstinacy."* But we should get in exchange a most interesting and racy character, with a great deal of human nature in it, a genial *bonhomie*, a bright wit, a love of society, especially that of cultivated ladies; a taste and talent for diplomacy of the sort that approaches intrigue; and an unaffected ardor of mystical devotion combining and co-operating with a practical shrewdness which made him a capital adviser of the pious but sentimental ladies who were his favorite correspondents, but which proved a dangerous gift to a man who had been taught by one of the most eminent Jesuits † connected

---

* See that tremendous piece of pulpit eloquence, the *Oration* of Bottini, Consistorial Advocate, at the canonization of Francis, transcribed in full by Father Morel.

† Father Possevin, author of the *Soldat Chrétien*.

with the affair of St. Bartholomew's Day, to make an unscrupulous use of it for the greater glory of God.

It is no wonder that a mind constituted like that of Francis should give early evidence of a vocation to the ecclesiastical career. It is not difficult to believe the story told of him that when other children were playing soldiers, he would be playing church, and leading about the little peasants in a procession instead of a battalion; nor that when he returned to his father's castle at Thörens in Savoy, from his costly education at Paris and Padua, an accomplished and brilliant young man of twenty-five, he should already have set before himself the position of Bishop and Prince of Geneva* as a more congenial one than any he would be likely to attain in the profession of arms, or in the career which his father's ambition had marked out for him, of country gentleman and senator of Savoy.

The story of the disappointment of the father's plans is told by the most voluminous and authoritative of the saint's biographers, the Abbé Marsollier, with a naïveté characteristic of that class of writers. Soon after Francis' return home, his father announced that he had arranged a marriage

---

* So the Abbé Marsollier, Vie de St. François, livre 1.

for him with a charming young heiress in the neighborhood, daughter to the Baron de Végy. "It struck the young count like a thunderbolt," says the biographer, who has been dwelling with delight on the early vows of celibacy which the young student had made in his private devotions; and yet not so much like a thunderbolt after all, but that he was quite willing to ride over to castle Végy and take a look at the young lady. In fact, a sense of respect for his father's wishes, or something, led him to call often on Mlle. de Végy, until *her* feelings, at least, had become very tenderly engaged. "This young lady" (we quote from the biography of Loyau d'Amboise) "no longer concealed from him how dear he had become to her. She never looked on him without an indefinable smile that bespoke the feelings of her soul. Not more soft were Rachel's sighs for Jacob, not more tender the looks with which she greeted his return to the roof of Laban after charming away the fatigues of the day with thoughts of her." To the great satisfaction of both families, the affair was looked upon as settled. Mutual congratulations were exchanged, and in the château de Sales they began to choose the place for the bride's portrait, and to talk about the arrangements for the wedding party. But either the young count had changed his mind in the course of the wooing, or, as his biographers proudly assert, he never had had the slightest intention of marrying the girl at all. At all events, while this billing and cooing was going on, the young saint was in consultation with his cousin Louis, canon of the chapter of Geneva, to get him neatly out of the affair, which was managed by securing for him from the Pope the most brilliant ecclesiastical appointment in the diocese, that of provost of the cathedral, that had just fallen vacant. Not till the document that secured him this prize was fairly in his hand did Francis take any step that could compromise his hopeful relations with Mlle. de Végy. The disappointment, mortification and shame of his parents, when he came to them in company with his cousin, the canon, showing the brief of nomination, and announcing his intention to accept it, are described with exultation by his panegyrists. His mother, with her woman's heart, pleaded tenderly for the forsaken girl. "Think," she said, "of her distress when she finds that you have jilted her, and that she is repelled by the heart that should have been her refuge and her love. Bitter will be her tears, for she has given you her heart *without the slightest mistrust.*" There was nothing to be alleged in answer to this appeal but his vow and his vocation, reinforced by certain miraculous indications of duty that were conclusive to his own conscience, but which, in the crude judgment of a man of the world, it would have been better to have forgotten altogether than to have recollected only at that stage of the affair. His mother, who seems to have a very clear view of the matter, merely answered: "This vow of yours was a very fine impulse; but you know just as well as I do that you could be released from it by a single word of the Bishop of Geneva."*

This incident in the life of Francis has no adequate justice done to it in the English biographies; but by the Abbé Marsollier and by Loyau d'Amboise it is detailed as a heroic instance of sacrifice for conscience' sake. In reading it, however, one can hardly resist the thought how near the young saint might have been, at the time, to a premature martyrdom to his principles; that if Mlle. de Végy had happened to have a big brother, the bodily sufferings of Francis for

---

* See the *Lives* of the Saint by the two authors cited. The complacency with which they tell the story so as to show all the essential facts, and yet without a suspicion that there is anything but heroism in their hero's course, is wonderful.

his devotion to the Church might have begun before he had so much as entered on his apostolic work among the fierce Protestants of the Chablais.

It is no more than justice to the memory of the saint to say that this seems to have been the most serious of the indiscretions into which he fell in his relations with the fair sex. The excessive protestations, on the part of himself and his clerical eulogists, of a very exceptional virtue in this regard, and his too frequent occasions for hand-to-hand encounter with temptation, such as do not usually occur to honest gentlemen who keep temptation at a proper distance, suggest suspicions for which there is no corroboration. He was eminently a ladies' man, "for ever surrounded by women;"* and he was evidently disposed by nature to a sort of coquetry, against which he doubtless strove to guard himself. The mild terms of almost playful rebuke with which he answers letters of amorous adulation are in bad taste; but bad taste is not always sinful, whatever Mr. Ruskin may say. The bishop writes, for instance, in 1618, to one of these enthusiastic adorers: "Dearest girl of my heart, I want to tell you that I have a child who writes to me that, being

---

* Spirit of St. Francis, III., 1, § 24, Ed. Rivingtons.

separated from me has thrown her into distress; that if she did not restrain her eyes they would shed tears over my departure, as the sky sheds rain, and other fine things of the sort. But she goes beyond this, and says that I am not a mere man, but some divinity sent on earth to compel us to love and admire him; and she even adds that she would use still stronger language if she dared. Now, my child, what do you think of that? Isn't it very naughty to talk so? Isn't it extravagant language?"* etc. Let him that is without sin rebuke the genial, warm-hearted bachelor bishop for not dropping that sort of letter into the fire unanswered, or for not answering it sharply. Our censure, if we should venture upon any, would be reserved for the editor who, in culling from the voluminous masses of the saint's correspondence, materials for a Complete Religious Letter-writer for English clergymen and their fair parishioners, should, out of so much that is admirable, have selected this one. It is withal an injustice to the character of Francis, who, in very trying circumstances, proved himself, we honestly think, as pure as the average of Protestant ministers—and that is high praise.

---

* *Lettre à une dame, du 22 avril*, 1618. P. 82 of the volume of Messrs. Rivingtons. Ed. Blaise, 418.

Of course no one will justify everything in his affair with Mme. de Chantal. We will not deny that a miraculous revelation from heaven* may justify, in extreme cases, a fascinating clergyman of thirty-seven in cultivating a platonico religious intimacy with an extraordinarily beautiful widow of thirty-two. But no case could justify the parties in clandestine correspondence such as took place at the outset of this aquaintance. It was June 14, 1604, that Francis wrote to the Baroness de Chantal: "Since your father-director permits you to write me sometimes, I beg you will do so freely and heartily. It will be an act of charity. My present circumstances and occupation make me an object of compassion. To hear from persons like you refreshes me like dew. The length of this letter shows you how my mind relishes intercourse with yours."† *This* letter was intended to be shown freely to her father and to her confessor, and contained expressions highly gratifying to their feelings. Ten days later it was followed by a strictly confidential letter, tending to supplant the influence of both these gentlemen by his own. "My last letter," he says,

---

* Francis himself makes no pretence of the heavenly vision.
† Letter of June 14, 1604. No. 58.

"will help you to quiet the mind of the good father to whom you ask leave to show it. I stuffed it well with things calculated to forestall any suspicion on his part that it was written with design;" and he goes on to urge her by the example of St. Teresa, not to limit her confidences to her confessor, but to accept him, Francis, in a more intimate and spiritual relation.* We really believe that much good came of this friendship with Mme. Chantal, especially as the parties grew older; and that no serious harm came of it, beyond some temporary distress in the family of President Frémiot, a revolting and fatal "marriage of convenience," and a certain amount of duplicity, and of unwholesome excitement in both the bishop and the baroness growing out of their unnatural relation. The affair turned out much better than it began. If any document nearly as scandalous as the letter above quoted had been produced in a recent *cause célèbre* in which the character of one of the most famous of modern preachers was at issue, it would have gone hard with him before the jury. We will not say more than that our saint was indiscreet; but it is impossible to say less: and the disposition to

---

* Letter 59.

dodges and intrigues illustrated by this incident throws a light on other portions of his history which it would not be honest to refuse to accept.

The character in which Francis has had least justice done him by the publications commonly current is that of *Missionary*. His greatest achievement, the conversion of the Chablais, is related copiously and effusively by Lady Herbert and more briefly by the author of *A Dominican Artist*. But the substance of the story, as they tell it, may be condensed into a few words. Being sent as a young man to destroy by his preaching the Protestant heresy that had become rooted in the province of the Chablais, he devoted himself to this task, in the face of excessive dangers and hardships, refusing military aid and protection, for the space of four years. The force of his arguments, the persuasiveness of his eloquence, the meekness and gentleness of his life, the sweetness of his disposition, his forgiving love towards his enemies, and the miracles that were wrought by him, overcame the bitter prejudices of the Protestants, who came to him in thousands to abjure their errors, until, by the influence of his ministry, the whole population of the province was won to the Church, and heresy completely extirpated.*

Thus runs the story; but the biographies of the saint, even in the mitigated form in which they are delivered to the British public, enrich this outline with magnificent colors. We are led by them through a bewildering haze of fictions and exaggerations. The project of canonizing Francis was entertained even before his death, and the work of procuring proofs of his sanctity was diligently begun by his influential family. The miracles of the saint are boldly compared to those of the Saviour of mankind, and under the one head of the raising of the dead are declared to be fully equal to those of the divine model.† But the wonders wrought by Francis himself are far below those effected by the imagination of his eulogists. Not only do they multiply the population of the province tenfold, but

---

* The most condensed summary of the fictitious legend of Francis de Sales is perhaps the Bull of Canonization, which may be found in the Appendix of the *Life* by Loyau d'Amboise.

† The original *Life of Francis*, published by his nephew Auguste, about ten years after the apostle's death, concludes thus, with almost inconceivable bad taste: "It is that son and nephew that Francis loved that testifieth of these things, and he knoweth that his witness is true. And many other things did Francis de Sales, which are not written in this book, which, if they were written, I believe that the world would not contain them." But it is a notable fact that with the single exception of the casting out of devils, not one of these miracles is mentioned or alluded to by Francis himself.

they change the face of nature and create
new heavens and a new earth for the scene
of their hero's exploits. The charming
plain on the southern shore of Lake Leman,
fenced from harsh winds by magnificent
walls of mountain, where fig trees grow in
the open gardens, and the gravest of the
winter hardships is the rarity of a week's
skating, becomes an awful wilderness in
which "eternal winter" reigns, such as
Salvator Rosa loved to paint. The quiet,
good-humored peasants are transformed into
fierce assassins, ambushed in every hedge ;
and the stalwart young apostle, " one of the
best built men of his time," flush of money
and resources of every kind, backed by the
treasury and army of Savoy, and perhaps
the best protected man in Europe, is
changed into a suffering martyr, confronting daily deaths with heroic resignation,
and answering the warnings and entreaties
of his friends with a calm, patient smile.
Everything becomes heroic. For better
security, he takes his lodging at the castle
of Allinges, on a pretty knoll of rock commanding a delicious landscape, where he is
the petted guest of the commandant; and we
are invited to admire the fortitude of this
stout, active young fellow of twenty-seven
in that he actually takes the hour's walk

into town on foot.* He has chilblains, and we hear (in the panegyrics) the gurgling of the blood as it gushes through his stockings and gaiters and stains his footprints in the snow. A bridge being broken, he crosses the stream on a plank; and his biographers roll their pious eyes and lift up adoring hands in admiration of the miracle. Later in his career, when as bishop he visits the valleys of Chamounix and Sixt, his admirers will not be content unless we join in their wonder at the sublime courage and self-denial with which he adventures himself in those dreadful places whither it is the delight of tourists from all the lands of the earth to follow him.†

When Francis de Sales entered on his mission in the Chablais, in September, 1594, that region had been Protestant for fifty-eight years. Thirty years before, in 1564, it had been receded to Savoy by the Bernese, in the treaty of Nyon, with the stipulation that the exercise of the Protestant religion

---

* In the *Life* by Loyau d'Amboise, the one league stretches to three "that the fatigue may touch hard hearts," p. 70, 72.

† Francis was a lover of natural beauty (see Sainte Beuve, *Port Royal*, I, 218) and fully capable of enjoying the magnificent scenery of his diocese. Mr. Gaberel, the venerable historian of Geneva, makes the curious remark in his work on *Rousseau et les Genevois*, that the earliest mention to be found in extant literature of the natural beauties of the region of the Leman is in Auguste de Sales' life of his uncle.

therein should not only not be molested, but should be protected and maintained by the Catholic sovereign — a stipulation allowed for the express reason that the people of the ceded province were so heartily attached to their faith that it would be impossible to detach them from it without great violence. Under this treaty the Chablais abode in peace and prosperity for sixteen years, until the death of the just and liberal-minded Duke who made the treaty, and the accession of his son, Charles Emmanuel, a prince the depth of whose religious convictions is indicated by his declaration that he held it to be " the duty of a good Christian to fight the Genevese, all pledges and oaths to the contrary notwithstanding." His deed was as good as his word. Plots of treachery and secret violence against the heretic city succeeded each other so frequently that at last the magistrates decided that a state of open war was better than such a peace; and in 1589 war was declared by the little town against its powerful and warlike neighbor— a war that horribly devastated the entire neighborhood, and drained Geneva of blood and treasure, but left it covered with glory and strong in religious faith. In the course of this war, Thonon, the capital of the Chablais, being attacked by the Genevese with their Swiss and French allies, surrendered, doubtless with small regret on the part of its Protestant population. When, at the beginning of an unstable peace, in 1694, the treaty of Nyon was reaffirmed, the Duke did not forget the coldness of the people of Thonon in the war against their fellow-believers, and had not long to wait for an opportunity of revenge.

That very year the Duke resolved to convert the Chablais. The time was well chosen. The people had suffered miserably in the war, and had little heart to resist injustice; the Protestant pastors had been harried out of the country, and only three or four of them allowed to return; public worship had ceased in most of the villages, and the children were growing up without instruction; little heroic Geneva crouched behind her walls, panting in utter exhaustion ; and what was more to the purpose, Berne, the other party to the treaty of Nyon, that had the right, under its terms, to insist on the maintenance of the stipulation in favor of the Protestant religion, had shown very plainly that she had no more stomach for fighting on account of others, so that there was little danger of any hindrance growing out of that document, unless it were, peradventure, some scruple of honor on the Duke's part, or some diplomatic remonstrance from Berne.

Accordingly the Duke sent a letter to the old Bishop of Geneva, at Annecy, asking him to send missionaries into the Chablais, and promising to aid them in their work with the whole force of his authority, to give them commissions accrediting them as employed in the ducal service, and to charge all commandants of posts to help the work to the utmost of their power. Perhaps the history of Christian missions has never offered an opening with so many attractions to an enterprising and devoted clergyman, and so few drawbacks, as that now presented to the brilliant and active young Provost of the chapter. Francis volunteered at once, and started for his mission-field without delay, accompanied by his cousin Louis, the canon.

He had every imaginable advantage for success in his enterprise—young, handsome, ardent and enthusiastic, noble of birth, bold and persevering, sustained by family influence that gave him admission to all the best society of the province, peculiarly insinuating in the society of ladies, quick-witted, diplomatic and adroit, rarely losing his temper in controversy, but maintaining the imperturbable suavity of his manner even when his practical operations were of the severest and cruellest; he was at the same time a man of strong convictions—strong, that is, with the strength that comes of an obstinate and conscientious resolution never to ponder an objection;* of graceful though effeminate eloquence; of intense mystical piety; and what proved in the end to be of even greater importance to his undertaking—a versatile readiness in applying means to ends without being embarrassed by squeamish scruples of honor and conscience. Leaving out of consideration the alleged miracles by which his work was aided, it might almost be said that if a man so gifted and so favored should not be successful in a good cause, it would be itself a miracle as great as some of those ascribed to him in the act of canonization.

Naturally, the mission organized under such auspices directed itself at once to the fortress of Allinges, the headquarters of the military governor of the province, from which, by means of a powerful garrison, he held in subjection not only the neighboring city of Thonon, but the whole of the harassed and wasted province. To him the missionaries presented their letters from the

---

*See, for a single instance, letter XI, p. 57. Ed. Rivingtons.

Duke enjoining him to render them all the
protection and support in his power. The
governor was just the man for the occasion.
A good Catholic, a zealous subject, a brave
and cruel soldier, the Baron d'Hermance
was also a family connection and an old
personal friend of the Apostle. A plan of
campaign was soon settled. They were to
begin with the mildest measures, reserving
the use of violence as a last resort.* This
was a course both congenial to the feelings
of Francis, and in accordance with the ideas
of the Duke, who was not without fears lest
his perfidy should provoke the Bernese to
armed interference. The old soldier further
advised the missionaries that it would be safer
for them to spend their nights at the fort.
The people of the Chablais, so he assured
them, were a good-natured, simple, rude
sort of folk, but very obstinate when they
had made up their minds; they had a very
bad opinion of the Roman Church, and
were convinced that their liberties and
privileges depended on their holding fast to
their religion—a notion that proved to be
not far from right. The next morning the
mission was appropriately inaugurated by a
review of the troops, and the governor,

* Marsollier, livre II.

pointing to his force of artillery, remarked significantly to Francis: "If the Huguenots over there will give you a hearing, I hope we shall have no need to use these guns."*

Advancing bravely from his fortified base, Francis presented himself to the magistrates of Thonon with letters commanding them to render all possible services to the missionaries, and to attend upon their preaching, and warning them that any injury offered to the priests would be avenged on the whole city of Thonon. The impression thus made may have been salutary, but the mild and inoffensive ways of Francis gave little provocation to violence. The presence of two such commissioners as he and his cousin naturally provoked a temporary agitation in the town, which, however, soon subsided, and the mission went on quietly but diligently. He was free to use the great church of St. Hippolyte, and there, day by day, he gathered the little handful of about a dozen Catholics, mostly strangers, to hear him preach. It was natural to expect that the uncommon attractions of the man himself, and the prodigious combination of influences by which he was backed, would at least win now and then a straggling towns-

---

* Thus the biographers generally; but the quotation is mitigated by English editors. Cf. Bull of Canonization. § 15.

man or peasant to listen to the famous preacher. But it was not so. He bewails his disappointment in successive letters. "We had hoped that some would come to hear us, either out of curiosity or out of some lingering love for the old religion. But they have all resolved, with mutual exhortations, not to do it."*— "Their heart is hardened. They have said to God: We will not serve thee. They will not hear us, because they will not hear God." And yet the governor had been as good as his word, and used his personal persuasions to induce persons to hear the Apostle. But the result is summed up by Francis in these words: "I have been preaching at Thonon now seven months on every holiday, and often in the week besides. I have never been heard but by three or four of the Huguenots, and these only came four or five times except secretly." Having utterly failed in drawing the people to hear him, he went down among the people, and taking his stand in the public square on market-days, attempted to catch their attention whether they would or no. This was equally in vain. The peasants were as ob-

* This and the following citations are from his letters of this period. In one of them Francis alleges that a municipal law was made forbidding attendance on his sermons. But this is very unlikely. In the Ed. Blaise (Paris, 1821) the letters may be found in chronological order.

durate as the citizens. In the country villages they refused not only to hear him, but even to give him so much as a lodging on payment. At the end of a year's toil, wishing to draw together all the results of his mission, he announced far and wide that he would preach on St. Stephen's day in a church near the Allinges. The concourse consisted of seven persons. Up to this time Thonon had not furnished a single convert. The father of Francis wrote to him that all the wisest and most sensible people considered his further persistence in the mission as a mere tempting of Providence, and that the only way to bring back such heretics to the faith was by the mouth of the cannon.

Nevertheless, with admirable persistence, Francis resolved to keep at it for another year, concentrating all his efforts on the town of Thonon. Already he had made use of the press to circulate his doctrines in little tracts and broadsides. He now devoted himself to discussions, private and public, and to the preparation of a book in exposition of Catholic doctrine. The aim of his teaching, both oral and printed, was characteristic of the man. It was conciliatory, dwelling on the points of resemblance between the two Churches, rather than on the points of difference, and seeking to produce the impression that the change from Protestant to Catholic, which would be attended by such vast worldly advantages, was not so difficult a matter as some were disposed to think. It was charged against him by some of his own brethren that he was not honest in this matter; and it is either very fortunate or very unfortunate for his reputation as a Catholic saint and doctor, that the book that would have settled the question—the book above mentioned—should completely and mysteriously have disappeared from the face of the earth.*

Finding townsfolk and peasantry as steadfast as ever in their faith, Francis turned to the provincial gentry. Helplessly dependent as these were on the duke's favor for promotion, whether in a military or in a civil career, it was not difficult to bring strong motives to bear upon them to persuade them to give a hearing to the message of salvation. Among them, the Baron d'Avully, a man of great influence, was the husband of a zealous Catholic lady, a devoted admirer of Francis. Her "prayers and tears," combined with the arguments of the missionary, made a deep impression

---

* This is all the more remarkable, since with the exception of this important work, every scrap of Francis' writing has been so religiously preserved.

on this gentleman; but before announcing his conversion he asked to hear a discussion of the points at issue. A meeting was arranged between Francis and Pastor La Faye of Geneva, at which the discussion lasted three hours. The affair being reported only by friends of Francis, it is needless to say that the wretched Protestant was overwhelmed with argument at all points; "frantic with rage, he broke out in a torrent of insulting language." It is again unfortunate that we have no report of the language used; but the papers of a subsequent discussion between the same parties are to be seen in the Library of Geneva, and afford us some ground of conjecture. To his antagonist's argument our saint meekly replies: "Your book is utterly worthless. It is packed with absurdities, lies, and blasphemies. It is the work of a poor, arrogant, broken-winded minister, who has gone crazy with passion and rage; a foolhardy, blind, impudent impostor, a charlatan, a Proteus, a chameleon, an excessively ignorant ex-monk and ex-priest." In answer to these gentle words, the heretic bursts forth with his furious insolence as follows: "I am not a Proteus nor a chameleon ever since I have known God's truth I have steadfastly followed it. It is a small matter to be judged of man's judgment. We must stand or fall to our own Master, to whom all our service is due. The Christian's fairest ornament is a humble mind. Let him that thinketh himself wise take heed lest he fall." If the above is an accurate report, it is truly painful to see how far the tender, gentle nature of the saint had changed places with such a rude creature as this Geneva pastor.*

Besides d'Avully, there was converted a noted lawyer named Poncet. Of these accessions the utmost was made. D'Avully was honored with a brief from the pope's own hand, couched in the most flattering terms, and assuring the neophyte of the distinguished favors of the duke. But the hopes inspired by these two successes were disappointed. At the end of the second year's toil, the list of converts amounted to just twelve,† and the disgusted apostle declares to the duke: "Your Chablais is a ruined province. Here have I been laboring twenty-seven months in this miserable country; but I have sown among thorns or in stony places.

---

* The citations are from Gaberel, *Hist. de l'Eglise de Genève*, II., 346. But the later editions of Francis' works are expurgated of insulting words and adapted to the modern taste. Ibid. 642.

† The list of them is given in the original Life by Auguste de Sales; but according to the current biographies the converts in Thonon alone were long before this to be counted by hundreds. See, for example, Loyau d'Amboise, p. 84.

Certainly, except M. d'Avully, and Poncet the lawyer, the rest of the converts are not much to talk of. I pray God for better luck; and I am sure that your highness's piety will not permit all our efforts to be in vain." *

For many months it had been growing plain to Francis and his friends that measures of a more vigorous sort must be used if anything was to be accomplished. This is the point of his appeal to the duke's piety. A year before, his friend President Favre had condoled with him on the inefficient support he received from the authorities; and the apostle himself had complained to the Jesuit Canisius that "His Serene Highness would not use violence to bring these people back into the Church, on account of the treaty on that point with Berne." But on December 29, 1595, he applies to the duke to have President Favre sent with a commission to compel the citizens to attend his preaching. "This gentle violence," said he, "will I think constrain them to accept the yoke of our holy zeal, and make a great breach in their obstinacy." †

---

* *Discours au Duc de Savoie le 9 décembre* 1596. Œuvres de St. François de Sales, Ed. Blaise, vol. XIV. Opuscules, p. 75.

† To this earlier period of the mission belong the stories of attempted assassination from which the saint escapes, sometimes by miracle and sometimes by "sweetness," but always magnificently scorning the protection of the secular arm. There is every reason to believe that they

So absolute was the necessity, that, notwithstanding the unfavorable season, he crossed the Alps in November, 1596, for a personal interview with the duke at Turin. The new program for the conversion of the Chablais which he submitted to the duke in council, is reported by Lady Herbert with great " sweetness " as consisting chiefly in " three things : the re-establishment of the mass at Thonon ; the restoration of the property belonging to the Church ; and the appointment of a certain number of priests and teachers, at fixed revenues throughout the province. He also urged the establishment of seminaries and schools ; the prohibition of heretical and atheistical publications ; and the foundation of a House of Mercy at Thonon." * Some trifling matters besides are contained in the memorandum of Francis, which have escaped her ladyship's

---

are all falsehoods. Francis never alludes to them. His parents at home did doubtless fidget about the safety of their favorite son. But a letter to him from his friend, President Favre, says : " My only trouble is that your good father worries so for fear some harm will come to you, that I can hardly persuade him that you are perfectly safe and that, as I believe, there is *not the slightest occasion to suspect danger* for you. I comfort him all I can, often protesting (what I am sure you do not doubt) that I never would have left you if I could have perceived *the slightest danger* to be feared." After Francis' death these assassination stories had a double value, as contributing to the materials of canonization, and as blackening the character of the Protestants.

* *The Mission in the Chablais*, p. 81.

attention, but which we add as an illustration of the saint's business-like ways:

"The minister of Thonon to be sent away to some place where he can have no intercourse with his people.

The heretic schoolmaster to be removed and a Catholic put in his place until the Jesuits can be settled.

Liberalities to be shown towards some seven or eight old persons who have remained Catholic.

Heretics, within a brief time, must be deprived of all public offices, and Catholics appointed into their places.

Good promotion in the army for Catholic young men.

One of the senators to summon all the citizens of Thonon to turn Catholic.

All Protestant books to be burned.

Your highness to show liberality to the new converts.

It is necessary to *scatter terror* through the whole population by wholesome edicts."*

The Council shrank from a policy at once

---

*See the copy of the original memorandum in *Etudes biographiques sur St. François*, Chambéry, 1860. This work, although published anonymously, is valuable and accurate. There is also a scholar-like and conscientious thesis by Pastor Guillot of the Geneva Church, entitled *François de Sales et les Protestants*, Genève, 1873. The two chapters on Francis de Sales in M. Gaberel's *Histoire de l'Eglise de Genève*, vol. II, have been violently attacked in a pamphlet by the Abbé Fleury (*magni nominis umbra*), entitled *St. François de Sales, le P. Chérubin et les ministres de Genève*, Paris, 1864. The writer clearly convicts his antagonist of some loose quotations, but leaves him safe in his main positions. These various documents will guide the student to the original sources of information.

so audacious and so perfidious. But "with his usual sweetness" (as the Abbé Marsollier admiringly puts it) the ardent young saint represented that the other party to the treaty was in no condition to enforce his rights; that the conversion was of great political importance; that he would not recommend using *violence* at all; but that "if the Council thought they were going to re-establish Catholicism in the Chablais with only such means as had been used hitherto, they were very much mistaken."

The Council were not convinced. Perhaps, indeed, the clergyman had failed to see the point of their scruples. But the duke, whose conscience was not over nice, had been won to Francis' policy in advance. He cleared the Council Chamber with a *sic volo, sic jubeo*, and the saint returned to his spiritual labors in triumph.

The first use which he made of his new powers must, we fear, be described as characteristic. Secretly, without communicating with the authorities of the town, he introduced workmen into the great church of St. Hippolyte, and commenced tearing down and building to transform the edifice into a Catholic church. This high-handed operation, begun without any show of authority, naturally provoked an indignant tumult.

The magistrates of the town hastened to the church, and restrained the people from violence; then turning to Francis they reminded him, with dignity, that under the treaty of Nyon theirs was a free city, and that such proceedings as his could not be undertaken but with their consent. Not until the affair had reached this point did Francis display his new orders from Turin to the eyes of the astounded and humiliated magistrates, with the threat that if they dared to interfere with them it would cost them the utter destruction of the town. It was, on the whole, not a pretty trick for an apostle to play; but it was fairly successful. It failed, indeed, to provoke a riot; but it succeeded in inflicting a public insult on the municipal authorities, and in "scattering terror" through the population. Francis wrote back to the duke with holy exultation: "The magistrates opposed me stoutly on the ground that it was a violation of the treaty of Nyon. I deny it: but even if it were a violation of the treaty, I do not see that it is any of their business."

But of what use was a church without a congregation? In order that the Christmas high mass should not be said to empty walls, President Favre went from village to village in the neighborhood "scattering terror" with one hand and seductive promises with the other. Under the assurance of being relieved from the crushing taxes, a number of the peasants were induced to attend the mass, and it was celebrated on Christmas day in the presence of these, and of the twelve Catholics of Thonon.*

From this time forth, Francis was aided by a great force of Capuchin friars and of secular priests, who were supported by the salaries that had been pledged by treaty to the exiled Protestant pastors. But our Apostle had lost faith in such means of evangelization, and looked for something more effective. Of any ordinary force there was no lack already in the garrisons of the Allinges and other military posts, which were under his orders, and which held the wretched country in complete subjection.† But there was need of something to "scatter terror"; and our saint knew of just the instrument for the purpose, if only he could

---

*Gaberel, II., 64, on the authority of a manuscript of the Capuchin friars who aided Francis. The manuscript is curious and of unquestionable authenticity; and I have taken pains to verify the citation. St. Genis (*Histoire de la Savoie*, II., 191) says that the mass was celebrated "before seven or eight old persons." This writer, showing no sympathy with the reformed religion, is nevertheless compelled to study the mission of Francis in its political and military aspects and comes to some very just conclusions.

*See Bull of Canonization, ? 16.

lay his hand upon it. The *Martinengo regiment* was a name that had only to be whispered in all that region to make the blood run cold with horror. It was a regiment of Spanish mercenaries that had been trained in the American wars to an exquisite delight and ingenuity in human torture. Seven years before, in the provinces neighboring the Chablais, it had been let loose like a ferocious beast by the Duke upon his own unarmed Protestant subjects, and day after day had revelled in ingenious torture, murder, and destruction. The simple *procès-verbal* containing the catalogue of these atrocities is one of the most awful pages in history. White-haired old men, the sick upon their beds, pregnant women, babies clinging to their mothers' breasts, were among the favorite objects of torture. To violate, to torture, to maim, to murder by slow degrees, were not enough; the bodies of the murdered must be mutilated and obscenely exposed. The village patriarchs were hung in their own chimneys to be slowly suffocated by the smoke. Others were dragged at the heels of horses, or roasted in burning barns, from which they were taken out gasping and thrown to die on dunghills. Meeting a young lad, the ruffians dislocated all his fingers, then filled his mouth with gunpowder and blew his head off. One of their commonest ways of inflicting a death of lingering anguish was of a sort that history refuses to describe. But the following incident of that brave campaign, from the *procès-verbal*, suffices to give an idea of the style of warfare of the Martinengo regiment:

"The 13th of September, 1589, the Duke of Savoy having the day before entered the province of Gex, his troops, passing through Crozet, took the Reverend Girard Barbier, minister of the Word of God at the said Crozet, aged about seventy-five years, split up the soles of his feet, and set him astride an ass, his face towards the tail, and led him thus, with every kind of insult, and beating him incessantly, to the Castle of Gex, and presented him to the said Duke, in whose presence he declared that he had preached nothing but the pure truth, and in the same would persevere until the end. And being brought away again, and thrown upon a little heap of straw in front of his house, he there died, all his goods having been pillaged."*

Evidently the Martinengo regiment was exactly what Francis needed for his apostolic

---

* See the document in full in Gaberel, II., Appendix 25. It fills eight pages of small type with a mere catalogue of horrors.

work. What he wanted was not soldiers, but those particular soldiers; and we need not say that his application for the use of them was not made in vain to that religious prince whom they had entertained by their playful treatment of the aged pastor of Crozet. At the Apostle's request, this horde of devils were billeted on the towns and villages of the Chablais. "Great was the people's surprise," says good Marsollier, "when they beheld the arrival at Thonon, without previous notice, of the regiment of the Count of Martinengo, lieutenant-general of the Duke's armies, who took lodgings in the town to await orders. The officers called in a body on Francis, and informed him that their orders were to do nothing except in co-operation with him."

From this point, the work of conversion was simple, straightforward, and rapid. The new missionaries showed great devotion to their work of confiscation and banishment. The earliest objects of their evangelic zeal were the three or four remaining pastors. Louis Viret, the infirm pastor of Thonon, took refuge across the lake, in the canton de Vaud. His colleague, Jean Clerc, was obliged to make his escape from the ruffians in haste with his seven little children, with no other provision than a piece of fifteen sons. Pastor Perrandet of Bons, quietly returning from a visit to a sick man, was overtaken by a trooper, who split his skull with a sabre.* Such acts as this last, it is to be hoped, were rare. Not many such could be necessary, and the saint disliked needless violence. All schoolmasters and other offensive characters were driven into exile.

Parallel with these persuasions were others of a kind more congenial to Francis' better nature. While obdurate Protestants were crushed with taxes, and saw their houses devoured, and their wives and daughters daily insulted by a billet of ruffianly troopers, the disinterested candor of those who showed themselves inclined to the new gospel was profusely rewarded by gifts, promotions, offices, festivities, and lavish hospitalities at the seats of the Catholic gentry. One noble house brought itself to the verge of ruin by its zealous liberality towards the new converts. A notable instance of the apostle's love to the household of faith was that of the minister Petit, made much of by all the saint's biographers as "a distinguished Protestant clergyman." The epithet does him less than justice. A dozen years before, he had

* Guillot, page 31.

been refused admission to the Geneva parishes for his infamous character. Only two years before, the pastors of Gex, believing him penitent, put him in charge of a village church; but at the end of a year he was deposed from the ministry, and afterwards lodged in gaol at Geneva, under accusation of various felonies, and narrowly escaped the gallows. In short, he was nearly as well known as Martinengo's troopers. Nothing was more natural than that he should have a sincere disgust for Protestantism; and Francis recognized without hesitation that he was just the man for his money, and had no scruple in writing to the Duke that this man could be had for a consideration. "This incomparable prince" promptly responded with an order on the treasury.*

But our apostle's burning thirst for souls was not yet satisfied. He had the aid of the Capuchins, the dragoons, the nobility, and Petit; and legions of miraculous powers attended him. But nothing would content him but he must have the Duke in person. In the autumn of 1598 his repeated importunities were fulfilled. In company with the cardinal-legate, De Medicis, the Duke approached the town of Thonon with vindictive feelings known to all, and restrained

---
*Gaberel, II, 612.

only by the frail bridle of his solemn word
and oath. The citizens and magistrates in
terror entreated the intercession of Francis.
It was a beautiful opportunity for the display of "his habitual sweetness." He put
himself, with the old bishop, at the head of
the Protestant magistracy and consistory,
marched out to meet the Duke, and threw
himself at his feet, refusing to rise until
the forgiveness of the citizens was granted.*
This *tableau* is said to have resulted in a
number of important conversions. But
touching as it was, it did not delay the saint
in getting to business. Some new articles
were all ready which he wished to have added
to his program of conversion. "The heretic
schoolmasters had been banished; now, let
no child be sent abroad to school. Let
heretics be expelled from all public offices,
not only in his highness' immediate service,
but in subordinate grades. Let Pastor Viret
be kept as far as possible from Thonon.
Let all Catholics dwelling in that town be
admitted to the *bourgeoisie*. Finally, let
all exercise of the Protestant religion be absolutely prohibited." † The Duke gave his
consent, and under date of the 12th of

---

* Abbé de Baudry, *Relation abrégée des travaux de
l'Apôtre du Chablais*, II.

* Gaberel, II., 625.

October, patents were drawn by which judges, advocates, attorneys, notaries, castellans, and other such functionaries were dismissed; and all their acts, subsequent to that date, were declared null and void; in short, the guaranteed liberties of the Chablais were destroyed by the stroke of a pen.* Ambassadors from Berne arrived soon after, with a protest against the perfidy; and the Duke submitted the matter to his Council, which advised him in favor of maintaining at least the show of good faith by tolerating the presence of three pastors in the province. But Francis warned the Duke under peril of everlasting damnation against any such weak concession,† and had his way about it.

The Duke was "amazed at the change that had passed over the people, and all the more so as no means had been used to bring them back to the Church but instruction and good example." Still, something remained to be done. How could this be, when the reported conversions already exceeded manifold the entire population of the country, is a materialist cavil easily disposed of in such an epoch of miracle. But for

---

* Œuvres de St. François, XIV., 91.
† *Life of Francis*, by Augustus, 179.

the hardened recusants who still held out against the sweetness of Francis, severer measures were now prepared.

One morning the gates of the town were occupied by soldiers of the Martinengo regiment. A double line of troops was posted in each of the principal streets, and the entire *bourgeoisie* of the town was summoned to present itself before the Duke in the great room of the Hôtel de Ville. With a shudder, the citizens observed that every exit from the room was guarded by these Spanish butchers,* and that at the right hand of the bloodthirsty Duke sat his inspiring genius in the person of the sweetly-smiling Francis de Sales. After a harangue addressed to the Protestants by a Capuchin friar, the Duke himself addressed them. He recalled the efforts that had been made for their conversion, not wholly without success. Those who had been converted would not fail of his royal favor. "But," said he, "there are those who are harder than the millstone; they love their wallowing in the mire; they prefer darkness to light. We detest them; and if they do not turn, they shall know what our disfavor

---

* The Abbé Marsollier chuckles with delight at the terror of the citizens who "believed that the Duke was about to proceed to the last extremities." *Vie de St. François,* liv. III.

means. Stand aside, wretched men! Let those that wear the Cross of Savoy in their hearts, and wish to be of the same religion with their prince, stand here at my right hand, and those who persist in their obduracy pass to my left!"

There was a moment of silence, a movement in the terrified crowd, and several went over and took their places at the right. But a large number still remained at the left. "Then the blessed Francis, leaving the Duke's side, came down among these, and exhorted them in the sweetest manner, saying: 'Are you not ashamed to act so? Have you no eyes nor senses? I warn you to look out for yourselves, for the Duke will show you no mercy.' Several were brought over by *these sweet words*. Then the Duke, turning toward the obstinate, cried: 'Depart from me! You are not fit to live. In three days begone from my territories!' The soldiers at once did their duty, and these wretched people went into exile toward Nyon or Geneva. There were among them gentlemen of good estate, and many of less importance. Then his highness put his patents into execution. The mass was re-established in all the churches, the offices taken away from the heretics, their books burned, and every one who would not accept the Roman religion was driven from the country." *

The "*coup d'état* of Thonon" was repeated by the same actors in all the villages of the Chablais. A later edict allowed six months for remaining heretics to choose between conversion and exile; and with this we may say that "the Mission in the Chablais" was concluded. Of course for long years to come, the like measures had to be renewed in order to prevent and punish relapse. Caresses and corruption diminished, indeed, but cruelty did not cease, and of all the protracted series of confiscations, banishments, and harryings, this smiling and seraphic creature, over whose inconceivable meekness and gentleness such libations of gushing eulogy are poured out by the British press, was the instigator, the director, and sometimes in his own person the executioner.†

---

* From the original *Life of St. Francis* by his nephew, quoted by M. Gaberel, II., 653. This work is the basis of all the subsequent biographies. The incautious *naïveté* of his statements is often modified by later authors, with a view to edification.

† On one occasion, some years after the *coup d'état*, two of the "converted" parishes were visited by ministers from Geneva "Francis, indignant at this temerity, hastened to the fortress of Allinges for an armed force, since treaties and plighted word availed nothing." [He never appears to so much advantage as when he is vindicating the faith of treaties.] "He obtained a detachment of soldiers, and thought right (since it concerned the cause of God) to put himself at their head, and drove out by physical force those whom he had often convinced by spiritual weapons." The story is told by Fremin, a renegade Genevese, who became *curé* of Russin, in his mss. *History of Geneva*, in the Geneva Library, p 510.

The work accomplished is variously estimated, according to the courage and imagination of the biographer. Loyau d'Amboise puts it at 20,000 converts. The Pope is very bold, and estimates Francis' total work of conversion at 70,000. Lady Herbert's discriminating pages give some elements for a conjecture, as by the 20,000 who shared in the adoration at the Duke's visit to Thonon, and the 162,000 communicants (it is well to be accurate) present at the Thonon Jubilee, "which put the finishing stroke to the work of conversion in the Chablais." The total population of this province, at the beginning of the mission, carefully estimated from censuses taken before and after, was less than 4000.*

One little incident closely connected with the conversion of the Chablais, is too characteristic to be omitted. There was living at the time, in Geneva, at the age of nearly eighty years, a most venerable man, the latest survivor of the company of the reformers, Theodore de Beza. The beauty and dignity of his old age charmed the great Casaubon, a few years later. "What a man he is!" he exclaims; "what piety! What

---

* The estimate is made by comparing the census of 1558 with that of 1694, Gaberel, II., 568. The splendid figure of 162,000 is inclusive of pilgrims who were present in large numbers.

learning! To hear him speak of sacred science, you could not believe him so extremely old. His whole life, his whole talk, is of God." He too, like Francis, was of noble birth, accomplished education, admirable gifts, beautiful courtesy of manner, and high devotion to religious duty. After a dissipated youth, he had received, with a penitence which all his after life attested, the teaching of the Holy Scriptures, to the unfolding of which his manhood was devoted. He left wealth and family behind him, gave up splendid benefices that were offered him in the Roman Church, and came to Geneva, where he became to Calvin what Melanchthon was to Luther. His whole life had been spent in stormy conflicts, but its eventide was full of peace and honors. By personal character, as well as by his position as presiding pastor of the Geneva Church, he was the foremost man of the reformed communion.

To Theodore de Beza, Francis de Sales was sent, during the unhopeful earlier months of his Chablais mission, with a commission from the Pope to labor for his conversion. Seeking private interviews with the venerable pastor, the enterprising young theologue plied him with arguments which (it is needless to say) were of small effect on the veteran colloquist of Poissy. Francis reported his ill-success to the Pope, and asked for further instructions. The instructions came; and this young gentleman was not ashamed to go back to the poor study in which the old man toiled at his daily work, with the offer, in the name of the Pope, of an annual pension of 4000 gold crowns, and a gift of twice the value of all his personal property, as the price of his apostasy. It is Francis himself that tells the shameful story, and adds that, seeing that he was accomplishing nothing, he withdrew and returned to Thonon. A contemporary manuscript, preserved at Geneva, adds that, at these insulting words, old Beza's gentle expression changed to sternness. He pointed to his empty book-shelves, whose precious contents had been sold to provide for the suffering refugees from France, and, opening the door for his guest, let him go with a *vade retro, Sathanas.**

* Nevertheless, the story that Beza was actually convinced and converted was studiously circulated at the time, and is repeated to this day in the Lives of Francis. On the grave authority of an after-dinner story told by a pot-companion of that chaste monarch, Henry IV., it is alleged that the cause which held this blameless old man to his principles was licentiousness! One may find the charge and the story gracefully reproduced by Lady Herbert, p. 97. The facts of the case, as any well-informed person might see, make the charge simply absurd. But it would be unjust to hold her ladyship to a rigid moral responsibility for lack of information. Beza was never under a vow of celibacy, so that there was not that to bind him even to the measure of self-denial exact-

To get possession of Geneva, and to be enthroned there, not only as bishop, but as secular prince, was one of Francis' earliest and latest dreams.* To what lengths of wrong-doing he was impelled by it, will not be known until the secrets of all hearts are revealed. He is known to us almost exclusively by the mendacious panegyrics of his friends, and by his own copious but not, ordinarily, incautious correspondence. Neither in these nor in other documents do we find anything to convict him of actual conscious complicity with the atrocious crime of the Escalade of 1602. What might have been if the perfidious projects which the Duke was continually nursing in his revengeful bosom had been rebuked instead of encouraged by his favorite clergyman, we can only guess. Perhaps it would have made no difference in the course of that wretched prince whom our saint publicly extols for his piety and for all the Christian

---

ed of the French ecclesiastic of the period. According to this story, he took refuge, for his vices, in the one corner of the earth where they were sure to be austerely and rigorously punished; and refused wealth and asylum in Italy where the state of society and law on this point was —what it was. It is interesting to read the Bull in which the Pope and two score Italian prelates put their virtuous hands to this d—graceful libel.

* Francis clung fast to the title of prince as well as bishop, to the day of his death; and his will, the autograph of which is shown, with other relics, at the family seat at Thorens, gives instructions for his burial in his own cathedral at Geneva, in case the town should be recovered to the Catholic religion after his death.

virtues, but whom, in a private conversation with Mother Angélique,* he denounces in a whisper for his "dirty tricks," as "clever in men's eyes but in the eyes of God a reprobate." Perhaps it might not have changed the Duke's course; but it would have been better for the memory of the saint.

The history of this prince's reign is stained on every page with plots to seize Geneva by perfidy, by purchased treachery, by ambuscade, by secret attack in times of plighted peace, under cover of assurances of his friendship; so that it was not with guileless unsuspicion as to what might be the bearing of the question, that Francis once answered his sovereign's inquiry: "What should be done with Geneva?"—"There is no doubt that heresy would be weakened throughout Europe if this town, the very seat of Satan, could be reduced and subjugated." And he went on to indicate at length the things that made this little town of 15,000 souls the metropolis and radiating centre of the reformed faith.

---

* Sainte Beuve (*Port Royal*, I., 257) quotes this discrepancy with admiration in proof of Francis' practical shrewdness and *finesse*. If it is right to speak of a saint as taking pride in anything, Francis was proud of his bluff, outspoken sincerity, "à l'ancienne gauloise."—"Je ne sais nullement l'art de mentir, ni de dissimuler, ni de feindre avec dextérité.... Ce que j'ai sur les lèvres, c'est justement ce qui sort de ma pensée,... je hais la duplicité comme la mort." Marsollier, liv. VIII, § 18.

Then, proposing certain spiritual methods, he added: "I know these remedies are small and slow, but is there anything else that could be done in this unhappy and degenerate age?" And then, in response to a word of encouragement from the Duke, he added slyly: "As to the *destruction* of the town, that is not exactly in my line nor to my taste. Your Highness has more expedients for that than I could dream of.* He conceals many things, but does not hide his feelings towards the city—*his* city, as he calls it—"that den of thieves and outlaws." He writes to the Pope: "This town is to heretics and devils what Rome is to angels and Catholics. Every good Catholic, but most of all the Pope and the Catholic princes, ought to do his best to have this Babylon demolished or converted."

Simultaneously with the preparations for the consecration of Francis as Bishop and Prince of Geneva, the Duke, stimulated by such talk as this from his spiritual adviser, carried on his secret preparations for that Escalade which, had it succeeded, would have anticipated, in the course of history, the horrors of the sack of Magdeburg by those of the sack of Geneva. It was plotted

---

* *Deuxième discours au Duc de Savoie.* Œuvres, XIV, 76.)

for the darkest night in the year, the 12th of December, o.s., 1602. About the end of November, Francis, returning thanks to the Chapter of his cathedral for their congratulations on his appointment, bade them: "Good-bye for the present, *expecting soon to meet you again in your own city.*" * Thence he went into retreat to prepare for the solemnities of his consecration. His confessor, on this occasion, was that noted Scottish Jesuit, Father Alexander, who stood a few nights later at the foot of the scaling-ladders and shrived the ruffians, one by one, as they crept up the wall of Geneva to their work of midnight assassination.† How the cruel and perfidious plot was foiled, and how the Duke slunk back to Turin foaming with disappointed rage, is it not told with glee in every Genevese family the world over, as often as the 12th of December comes round? One of the exasperating sights that met the Duke's eye as he rode homeward through Annecy, was the long train of sumpter-mules sent by his orders from Turin, laden with church decorations and altar furniture and with eighty hundredweight of wax candles, to be used

---

* Letter 42.

† This fact has recently been developed by Mr. Th. Claparède in a paper read before the Archæological Society of Geneva.

in the decoration and illumination of St. Peter's at Geneva, when its prince-bishop should celebrate mass at Christmas in his own cathedral church.

It is possible that for fear of displeasing the saint's "sweetness," these preparations had all been concealed from his too sensitive mind: that he had no conjecture about the mysterious movement of troops through his diocese; that his remark to his canons had no reference to anything in particular; and that the new bishop, looking out of his window at Annecy at the train from Turin, wondered in his heart where in the world all that church gear could be going to. We should wrong his blessed memory if we were to say that his guilt was demonstrated. But many a wretch has justly been hanged on less evidence of complicity in less atrocious crime.

It is not needful to pursue further the course of the life of Francis de Sales. The traits manifest in his earlier life (though veiled in most of his recent biographies) are to be recognized in all his subsequent career.* It would be easy, if only the torrent

---

* His labors in the Pays de Gex were quite of the same character with those in the Chablais, except that, instructed by his two years' experiment in the Chablais, he scattered no more of his rhetorical pearls before swine, but began at once with force. See Claparède, *Histoire des Églises reformées du Pays de Gex:* Brossard, *Histoire*

of fulsome panegyric would assuage long
enough to give the opportunity, to present
his character in more pleasing aspects.
There were noble and beautiful things in
Francis. But one tires of seeing this adroit
and courtier-like fanatic, with his duplicity
and his cold-blooded cruelty, recommended
in standing advertisements to the abused
public as "a model of Christian saintliness
and religious virtue for all time," as having
lived " a life as sweet, pure, and noble as
any man by divine help has been permitted
to live upon earth;" and as having been
"admirable for his freedom from bigotry in
an age of persecution." Neither can we
enter fully into sympathy with those to
whom "it is a matter of entire thankfulness
to find a distinctively Anglican writer setting forward " the ferocious and perfidious
dragonnades by which he extinguished
Christian light and liberty in the provinces
south of Lake Leman, and smote that lovely
region with a blight that lingers on it visibly
until this day, "as a true missionary task to
reclaim souls from deadly error, and bring
them back to the truth." * That writer

politique et religieuse du Pays de Gex : Bourg-en-Bresse,
1851; Guillot, *Fr de Sales et les Protestants :* Genève, 1873.
The legendary story of the mission in Gex may be read in
any of the Lives of Francis.

* The quotations are from " Opinions of the Press," in
Messrs. Rivingtons' Catalogue.

would render a good service, not only to history, but to practical religion, who should give the world a true picture of Francis de Sales, with all his singular graces and with his crying faults; and so supersede the myriads of impossible fancy-portraits with nimbus and wings, with eyes rolling in mystical rapture, and with the everlasting smirk of "sweetness" and gentleness.

HOW THE REV. DR. STONE BETTERED HIS SITUATION

HOW THE REV. DR. STONE BETTERED HIS SITUATION.

THE following argument, not less timely now than when it was first called forth by the publication of Dr. Stone's book, treats of the claims of the Roman Catholic Church from a neglected point of view, but a point which commands a much wider and juster view of the Roman system than the point commonly occupied by Protestant controversialists.

For many generations it has been a standing accusation against the Roman Catholic Church that it has a tendency to demoralize society and the individual by issuing certificates, written or oral, of the forgiveness of sins, and of the remission of the penalties of them, both in this world and the world to come, on the performance of rites, or the payment of money, or on other conditions different from those required in the gospel—repentance and faith.

In answer to this accusation, the apologists of the Roman Church have constantly averred, sometimes with a great show of indignation, that these certificates of forgiveness of sin and remission of penalty and assurance of salvation do not mean, and are well understood not to mean, what their terms import; that the understanding is distinct and explicit between the Church and its devotees, that when the priest says, "I absolve thee," he does not in fact absolve at all, and that the forgiveness of the "penitent," to whom these words have been pronounced in the confessional, is just as entirely contingent on his true repentance as the forgiveness of any sinner outside of the Church can be; that the promise given in an "indulgence" of the remission of purgatorial torment, notwithstanding it may be absolute in form, is really subject to similar conditions; and that the grace to be conferred, *ex opere operato*, by the sacraments generally, is in like manner dependent on such and so many contingencies, as to preclude the danger that any person will be tempted into sin by assurance of safety; that, if at any time, impenitent persons have been induced by the agents of the Church to purchase indulgences promising to remit the penalties of their sins, these promises, given by her agents in her name, are indignantly disavowed and repudiated by the

Church although there is no recorded instance of the money being refunded.

On the other hand, however, an opposite style of address is sometimes taken up by this Church and its advocates—a style of address calculated to assure those who have thought themselves shut up to the gospel promises of forgiveness on condition of repentance and faith—that there is something a great deal more certain and assured to be had in the Church of Rome; that her clergy have a peculiar power of binding and loosing, which other clergymen do not possess; that there is a gracious virtue in her sacraments, which cannot be found in others; that her pope, especially, has control over the keys of the kingdom of heaven. There is much in the tone of her teachings, in the language of her sacraments, and in the terms of her indulgences and other documents that corresponds with these pretensions. They are summed up in the persuasive language of Pope Pius IX, in his letter of September 13, 1868, addressed to Protestant Christians, in which he implores them to "rescue themselves from a state in which they cannot be assured of their own salvation," and come into his fold, where, as he implies, they can be assured of it.

These two "Phases of Catholicity," contradictory as they are, do, nevertheless, belong to the same system. And many a luckless polemic, reasoning from one set of the utterances of the Church of Rome, has been suddenly overwhelmed with the Virtuous Indignation and Injured Innocence with which his antagonists have confronted him with the other set of utterances, crying out upon him, "Is it Honest to say thus and so, when here are passages in our books or facts in our American practice which say just the contrary?"

If the Church of Rome could be driven up to choose between its two contradictory doctrines, the remaining controversy would be a short one. But this is hopeless. It clings inexpugnably to the fence, ready to drop on either side for the time, as the exigencies of controversy may require. It moves to and fro in its double-corner on the checker-board, and challenges defeat.

In the representations which I have occasion to make, of the Roman Catholic theology, I shall draw from the most trustworthy sources, giving full references in the margin. And I do not despair, in the more Christian temper which we thankfully recognize, in recent years, as governing both sides of the controversy, of finding that candid scholars on the opposite side acknowledge that I have written with at least honest and sincere intention, and that, albeit under a gently satiric form, I have a sober argument to submit which is worthy of a serious answer—if indeed there is any answer to be made.

One word more before coming to the argument. I wish to disclaim any personal disrespect for the gentleman whose name is used in the title of this article, and whose book is the text of the discussion. His theological position is demonstrably preposterous; but there is nothing else about him that is not worthy of all respect.

Dr. Stone's book, "The Invitation Heeded,"* was written in explanation and vindication of his sudden going over from the Protestant Episcopal to the Roman Catholic Church, just before the Vatican Council. Without criticising it in detail, we propose rapidly to state the upshot of the Rev. Dr. Stone's religious change, as it appears to us, and to foot up the balance of spiritual advantage which he seems to have gained by it.

In October, of 1868, the Rev. James Kent Stone, D.D., a minister of excellent

---

* *The Invitation Heeded:* Reasons for a Return to Catholic Unity. By James Kent Stone, late President of Kenyon College, Gambier, and of Hobart College, Geneva, New York; and S.T.D. Catholic Publication Society. 1870. 12mo, pp. 341.

standing in the Protestant Episcopal Church, received, in common with the rest of us, a copy of a letter from the pope of Rome, in which he was affectionately invited to "rescue himself from a state in which he could not be assured of his own salvation," by becoming a member of the Roman Catholic Church, which teaches, by the way, that as soon as a man becomes "assured of his own salvation" it is a dead certainty that he will be damned.*

Accordingly, the Rev. Dr. Stone, deeply conscious how uncertain and perilous is the position of those who merely commit themselves in well doing, with simplicity and sincerity, to the keeping of the Lord Jesus Christ according to his promises, "hastens to rescue himself from that state, in which he cannot be assured of his own salvation," and betters himself wonderfully as follows:

1. His first step is to make sure of his regeneration and entrance into the true church by the door of the church, which is, according to his new teachers, not Christ, but baptism.† To be sure he has once been baptized, and the Council of Trent warns him not to dare affirm that baptism admin-

---

* Act. Conc. Trid., Sess. VI., Cap. IX., XII., XIII.
† Concil. Florent., " vitæ spiritualis janua."

istered by a heretic (like his good old father) is not true baptism.* But as all his everlasting interests are now pending on a question which no mortal can answer, to wit, whether at the time of the baptism of little James, being then of tender age, the interior intention of old Doctor Stone corresponded with a certain doubtful and variously interpreted requirement of the Council of Trent—that he should "intend to do what the Church does"†—it is well to make his "assurance of salvation" doubly sure, by a "hypothetical baptism" from the hands of a Roman Catholic priest, with some accompaniments which although " not of absolute necessity to his salvation, are of great importance"— such as a little salt in his mouth to excite "a relish for good works," a little of the priest's spittle smeared upon his ears and nostrils to " open him into an odor of sweetness," a little of the essential " oil of catechumens" on his breast and between his shoulders, and of the "oil of chrism " on the crown of his head, with a "white garment " on, outside of his coat and pantaloons, and a lighted candle in his hand in the daytime.‡ If there is a way of meriting

---
* Concil. Trid., Canon 4, De Bapt.
† Concil. Trid., Ses. VII., Can. II.
‡ See the Roman Catechism.

heaven by a process of mortification, we have little doubt that it must be for a respectable middle-aged gentleman who has learned, by being president of two colleges, the importance of preserving his personal dignity, to be operated upon in just this way. Nothing, we should imagine, could add to the poignancy of his distress, and consequent merit, unless it should be to have the members of the sophomore class present while he was having his nose "opened into the odor of sweetness."

Doubtless the object to be gained is amply worth the sacrifice, since it is to "rescue oneself from that state in which he cannot be assured of his own salvation," and avoid that "eternal misery and everlasting destruction," which, according to the authoritative catechism of the Roman Catholic Church, is the alternative of valid baptism. This second ceremony, be it remembered, is only a hypothetical one, calculated to hit him if he is unbaptized; but, in case it should appear in the judgment of the last day that old Dr. Stone had intended to "do what the church does" (it being, at present, not infallibly settled what such an intention is), then this latter and merely hypothetical ceremonials is to be held to have been no baptism at all, but null and void to all intents and purposes whatsoever. But considering that the issues of eternity are pending on the insoluble question as to the validity of the first baptism, considering that a defect here can never be supplied to all eternity, whether by years of fidelity in other sacraments, or by æons of torture in purgatorial fire, since it is only by baptism that "the right of partaking of the other sacraments is acquired,"* it is nothing more than common prudence to adopt a course that diminishes by at least one-half the chances of a fatal defect. It must be admitted that there still remains a possibility of the defect of intention in the second act as well as in the first; such things having been known in ecclesiastical history as the purposed "withholding of the intention" in multitudes of sacramental acts on the part of an unfaithful priest. Still, it may be held, perhaps, by the Rev. Dr. Stone, that the hypothetical transaction makes the matter nearly enough certain for all practical purposes (as the old arithmetics used to say), although it falls a good deal short of that "assurance of his own salvation" to which he was invited in the pope's letter.†

But presuming that between his two bap-

* Dens, De Bapt. Tract.at
† It is very pleasant, from time to time, as one traverses the dreary waste of "commandments contained in ordinances" which make up the Romish system, to come

tisms Dr. Stone is validly entered into the Roman Catholic Church, may we not now congratulate him on the (hypothetical) assurance of his own salvation? Not quite yet. To be sure, he has received the remission of all his sins, up to that time, both original and actual, and the remission of the punishment of them, both temporal and eternal, and has been (as the Holy Father promised in his letter of September, 1868, already quoted) "enriched with unexhausted treasures" of divine grace.* But it is damnable heresy not to acknowledge that "he may lose the grace," or to hold "that it is possible for him to avoid all sins—unless by special privilege from God, such as the church holds to

upon some admission or proviso which, fairly interpreted, nullifies all the rest. The Council of Trent, for instance, declares that "without the washing of regeneration (meaning baptism), *or the desire of it*, there can be no justification," and teaches that an unbeliever brought to embrace Christianity, not having the opportunity of baptism but yet desiring to receive it, is "baptized in desire" —the desire supplying the place of the actual sacrament. (See Concil. Trident, Sess. VI., Can. 4; Sess. VII., Can. 4. Also Bishop's Hay's "Sincere Christian," vol.1, chap. xx.). It is obvious enough that the just interpretation and application of these very Christian teachings would blow the "doctrine of intention" and of the "opus operatum" to pieces. But the thorough-going Romanizers scorn to take advantage of such weak concessions. Cardinal Pallavicini says decidedly, "There is nothing repugnant in the idea that no person in particular, after all possible researches, can come to be perfectly sure of his baptism. Nobody can complain that he suffers this evil without having deserved it. God, by a goodness purely arbitrary, delivers the one without delivering the other." (Quoted in Bungener's "History of the Council of Trent," p. 159.) This line of argument will be of no small comfort to Dr. Stone in his disappointment about the "assurance of his own salvation."

* Catech. Roman., 152-169.

have been granted to the Blessed Virgin."*
Grace may come and go, but orthodoxy
agrees with experience in teaching that
"concupiscence, which is the fuel of sin, remains."† It is damnable, therefore, to
affirm that the rest of the seven sacraments
are not necessary to Dr. Stone's salvation ; ‡
and especially to affirm that "it is possible
for him if he shall fall" (as he inevitably
will) "after baptism, to recover his lost
righteousness without the sacrament of penance."§ which is "rightly called a second
plank after shipwreck;"‖ and equally damnable to "deny that sacramental confession
is necessary to salvation :"¶ or to "affirm
that in order to receive remission of sins in
the sacrament of penance it is not necessary,
jure divino, for him to confess all and every
mortal sin which occurs to his memory after
due and diligent premeditation—even his
secret sins."**

We find, therefore, that our estimable
friend is very, very far indeed, up to this
point, from having got what he went for.
He thought he was stepping upon something solid, but finds himself all at once in

---

* Concil. Trident., Sess. vi., Can. 23.
† Catech. Roman., ubi supra.
‡ Concil. Trident., Sess. vii., Can. 4.
§ Ibid., Sess. vi., Can. 29, De Justif.
‖ Ibid., Sess. xiv., Can. 2.
¶ Ibid., Sess. xiv., Can. 6.
** Ibid., Sess. xiv., Can. 7.

great waters, and making a clutch at the "second plank after shipwreck."

A certain embarrassment attends him at his first approach to the sacrament of penance. He has a distinct understanding with the church that all sins incurred before baptism, both original sins and actual sins, and all the punishment of them, both eternal punishment in hell and temporal punishment in this world or in purgatory, are absolutely and entirely remitted in that sacrament, and that no confession or penance is due on their account.*

But now the painful question arises, When was he baptized? He may well hope that the transaction of his good old heretic of a father and of his sponsors in baptism, when they called him M. or N., was only an idle ceremony; for in that case the long score of his acts and deeds of heresy and schism all his life through is wiped out by the hypothetical baptism, and he may begin his confessions from a very recent date. But if his father had the right sort of intention, then this hypothetical baptism is no baptism at all, and he is to begin at the beginning with his penance. Inasmuch as neither man nor angel can settle the question, he will act wisely to fol-

---

* Catech. Roman., ubi supra.

low the safe example of St. Augustine, and begin his confessions with owning up frankly to the indiscretions (to use the mildest term), with which, in early infancy, he aggravated the temper of his nurse, and peradventure disturbed the serenity of his reverend parent. Doubtless it will make a long story, but what is that, when one is seeking for the " assurance of his own salvation "? And oh the joy—the calm, serene peace—when he shall hear at last from the lips of the duly accredited representative of the church the operative sacramental words, *Ego absolvo te*, and know at last, after all these forty or fifty years of painful uncertainty, that at least for this little moment he is in a state of forgiveness and peace with God.

But softly! We are on the very verge, before we think of it, of repeating that wicked calumny upon the Roman Catholic Church against which Father Hecker so indignantly protests, saying:

"Is it Honest to persist in saying that Catholics believe their sins are forgiven, merely by the confession of them to the priest, without a true sorrow for them, or a true purpose to quit them—when every child finds the contrary distinctly and clearly stated in the catechism which he is obliged to learn before he is admitted to the sacraments?" *

Of course, it is not honest! We have not examined the catechism in question, for the reason that if we were to quote it against the church of Rome we should be told that it was not authoritative, and be scornfully snubbed for pretending to refer to what was not one of their standards—but of course it is conclusive against our honesty when they quote it. To be sure, the priest says in so many words: "I absolve thee from thy sins, in the name of the Father, and of the Son, and of the Holy Ghost;" and Bishop Hay, in a volume commended by the proper authorities to the confidence of the faithful, declares that "Jesus Christ has passed his sacred word that when they (the priests) forgive a penitent's sins by pronouncing the sentence of absolution upon him, they are actually forgiven."† But then nothing is better established than that these authorized books of religious instruction may be repudiated at discretion as of no authority at all, whenever the exigency requires it. Then the Catechism of the Council of Trent says in terms: "Our sins are forgiven by the absolution of the priest;" ‡ "the absolu-

---
* Tract of the Catholic Publication Society.
† Sincere Christian, Vol. II., p. 69.
‡ Catech. Roman, p. 289.

tion of the priest which is expressed in words, seals the remission of sins, which it accomplishes in the soul;"* "unlike the authority given to the priests of the old law, to declare the leper cleansed from his leprosy, the power with which the priests of the new law are invested is not simply to declare that sins are forgiven, but as ministers of God, really to absolve from sin." † Thus the Catechism of the Council of Trent; but bless your simple soul! it is not the Catechism of the Council that is infallible, but only the Decrees of the Council; and although these do, in their obvious meaning, seem to say the same thing, nevertheless Dr. Stone will find, when he comes to search among them in hopes to "read his title clear" to divine forgiveness on the ground of having received absolution from the priest, that what they say is qualified by so many saving clauses, and modified by so many counter-statements, that the seeker for the assurance of his own salvation is as far as ever from being able to

"bid farewell to every fear,
And wipe his weeping eyes."

Only one thing is absolutely certain : and that is that it is impossible for him to be

---

* Ibid., p. 240.
† Ibid., see the various Canons of Sessions vi. and xiv., of the Council of Trent, above quoted.

forgiven without absolution; but whether he is forgiven, or is going to be, now that he has received his absolution, does not by any means so distinctly appear. For "if he denies that in order to the entire and perfect forgiveness of sins, three acts are required in the penitent, to wit, Contrition, Confession, and Satisfaction, he is to be Anathema,"* which, if we understand it correctly, is quite another thing from being forgiven and assured of his salvation. Now Contrition, according to the same infallible authority, "is the distress and horror of the mind on account of sin committed, with the purpose to sin no more." "It includes not only the ceasing from sin, but the purpose and commencement of a new life and hatred of the old." † It is "produced by the scrutiny, summing up, and detestation of sins, with which one recounts his past years in the bitterness of his soul, with pondering the weight, multitude, and baseness of his sins, the loss of eternal happiness, and the incurring of eternal damnation, together with the purpose of a better life." ‡ Now it is important for Dr. Stone to understand (as doubtless he has been told by this time) that although this

---

* Conc. Trid., Sess. xiv. Can. 4.
† Ibid., Sess. xiv., Cap. 4
‡ Ibid., Sess. xiv., Can. 5.

will be of no avail to him without the absolution, or that at least the desire for the absolution,* nevertheless the absolution will be of none effect unless the contrition shall have been adequately performed.

Furthermore, a second part of the sacrament is confession, and there is an awful margin of uncertainty about this act; for it is damnable to deny that "it is necessary, *jure divino*, in order to forgiveness of sins, to confess all and every mortal sin which may be remembered after due and diligent premeditation."† But which of his sins are mortal and which venial, it is simply impossible for the Rev. Dr. Stone to know by this time, for it is a life's labor to learn the distinctions between them from the theologians, and when you have learned the distinctions, you have no certainty about them, for they never have been infallibly defined, and the doctors disagree. It may be tedious, but it is obviously necessary, in order to the assurance of his salvation, for the doctor to make a clean breast of all the sins, big and little, that he may remember "after due and diligent premeditation." But what degree of premeditation is "due" and "diligent" is painfully vague, consider-

---

† Ibid., Sess. xiv., Cap. 4.
* Ibid., Sess. xiv., Can. 7.

ing how much is depending on it. It were well he should give his whole time and attention to it. But even then he would be unable to judge with exactness when it was accomplished.

"Exactly so!" doubtless the Rev. Dr. Stone would say: "and herein consists the happiness of us who have 'rescued ourselves from the state in which we could not be assured of our own salvation'—that we have the advantage of a divinely authorized priest, with power of binding and loosing, who shall guard us from self deception and mistake, and certify us with sacramental words that all these uncertain conditions are adequately fulfilled, and assure us, in so many words, that our sins are remitted. Oh, the comfort of this distinct assurance from the Church!—this blessed sacrament of penance!—this second plank after shipwreck!"

Poor man! He has learned by this time that his priest does not undertake to certify him of anything of the sort—that the absolution is pronounced on the presumption that his own part of the business has been fully attended to, but that if his contrition or his confession has been defective, that is his own look-out, and he must suffer the consequences, even be they everlasting perdition. The absolution, in that case, does not count at all.*

"But," thinks the Rev. Dr. Stone, a little concerned about the assurance of his salvation, "if all the issues of eternal life are to turn on a question of my own consciousness, of which no one is to judge but myself, I do not see how I am so much better off on the point of assurance than when I was a Protestant, and had the distinct, undoubted promise of the Lord Jesus Christ himself of salvation on condition of repentance and faith." We feel for the honest man's disappointment, but can only recommend to him, in his present situation, to carry his trouble to his new

---

* "As the Church may sometimes err with respect to persons, it may happen that such an one who shall have been loosed in the eyes of the Church, may be bound before God, and that he whom the Church shall have bound may be loosed when he shall appear before Him who knoweth all things." Pope Innocent III., Epistle ii., quoted in Bungener's "History of the Council of Trent." We beg pardon for citing the language of a pope as an authority, since it is recognized on all hands that hardly anything is more unauthorized and fallible than the sayings of a pope, excepting only on those occasions when he speaks ex cathedra—and precisely when that is, no mortal can tell with certainty.

Let us try what a cardinal will say: "Without a deep and earnest grief, and a determination not to sin again, no absolution of the priest has the slightest worth or avail in the sight of God; on the contrary, any one who asks or obtains absolution, without that sorrow, instead of thereby obtaining forgiveness of his sins, commits an enormous sacrilege, and adds to the weight of his guilt, and goes away from the feet of his confessor still more heavily laden than when he approached him." Wiseman on the Doctrines of the Church, vol. ii., p. 10.

There would seem to be nearly the same amount and quality of comfort for tender consciences, and "assurance of salvation" here, as may be found (for example) in "Edwards on the Affections."

advisers. The best advice they can give him will perhaps be that which certain other high ecclesiastics, of unquestionable regularity of succession and validity of ordination once gave to a distressed inquirer—"What is that to us? see thou to that!"

It begins to look extremely doubtful whether we shall be able to get the Rev. James Kent Stone to heaven at all, on this course, notwithstanding he has come so far out of his way to make absolutely sure of it. But supposing all these difficulties obviated, and that by a special revelation (it is impossible to conceive of any other means of coming at it) he discovers that his baptism and contrition and confession are all right, and furthermore that the priest has had the necessary "intention" in pronouncing the absolution, and supposing a number of other uncertainties incident to this way of salvation, but which we have no time to attend to, to be entirely obviated, how happy he must be, *post tot discrimina tutus*, assured of the forgiveness of all his sins, and how delightful the prospect set before him—

"Sweet fields arrayed in living green.
And rivers of delight!"

Alas, no! If the Rev. Dr. Stone has any idea as this, it is only a remnant of the crude notions which he picked up in the days of his heresy, by the private interpretation of the Scriptures. Let him now understand that it is damnable error to hold "that when God forgives sins he always remits the whole punishment of them."* The eternal punishment, indeed, is remitted ; but the temporal punishment which remains to be executed may reach so far into the world to come that it is impossible to predict the end of it. In fact, the characteristic vagueness in which all the most important matters that pertain to one's salvation are studiously involved in the Roman Catholic Church is remarkably illustrated in this matter of purgatorial torment. The nature of it is doubtful. The majority of theologians hold that it is effected by means of literal, material fire—but that is only "a pious opinion," and will not be known for certain until the next time the pope speaks "out of his chair." The degree of it is doubtful. St. Thomas Aquinas thinks that it exceeds any pain known in his life ; Bonaventura and Bellarmine guess that the greatest pains in purgatory are greater than the greatest in this world ; but they are inclined to think that the least of the pains is not greater

---

* Concil. Trident., Sess. xiv., Can. 12. See also Sess. vi., Can. 30.

than the greatest in this world.* But the duration of purgatorial torment is the most uncertain thing of all. Some think it will last only a little while; others that it will endure for years and ages. The Church either don't know, or won't tell. The most distinctly settled thing about the whole business seems to be this: that no one was ever yet known to be delivered from purgatory so long as there was any more money to be got out of his family by keeping him in.

Is it not, now, rather a rough disappointment to a man who has done so much, and travelled so far, on the promise of a clear and "assured" view of his future happiness, to bring him through all those perils to the top of his Mount Pisgah, and bid him look off on a—lake of fire and brimstone? We put it to the pope, in behalf of our deceived and injured fellow-citizen—is it the fair thing?

Well, after all, ten thousand years of purgatory, more or less, will not so much matter to our friend, so long as he is "assured of his own salvation" from eternal perdition. Ay; there's the rub. He is not assured. Supposing it is all right thus far, with his baptism and confirmation and penance (and we have not stated a half of the diffi-

---

* Dens, De Purgatorio.

culties of this supposition), he is now indeed in a state of grace, and all his sins are forgiven, albeit part of the punishment of them is liable still to be inflicted in purgatory. If he dies now, happy man! for (always supposing as above) he is sure of being saved, sooner or later. But he has no certainty of remaining in this state of grace for an hour. And the Church (kind mother!) has provided for the security of her children by other sacraments, notably the sacrament of the Eucharist. Dr. Stone has undoubtedly, in his heretic days, read the sixth chapter of John, with the query, What if the Roman interpretation of these promises is the true one, and in order to have eternal life, I am required to eat the flesh and drink the blood of the Son of Man, literally, in the transubstantiated bread and wine; and he now recalls the Lord's promise, "if any man eat of this bread he shall live forever?"*—and he finds no small comfort in it. It is not pleasant to discover, indeed, that the Church, even granting the interpretation of the passage, declares it of none effect, giving it to be understood that thousands upon thousands have eaten the veritable "body and blood, soul and divin-

---

* John vi., 51; also 58.
"Whoso eateth my flesh and drinketh my blood hath eternal life."
Ibid., vi., 54

ity" of the Lord, and gone, nevertheless, into eternal death. But yet your "anxious inquirer" does seem to come nearer now to what he was looking for—a sacrament that shall do its saving work on him independently of the presence of that, the necessity of which casts a doubt on all Protestant hopes—faith on the part of the partaker. This is the satisfaction of the doctrine of the *opus operatum*, that it makes the saving virtue of the sacrament to depend, not on what it is difficult for the recipient to ascertain—his own faith; but on what it is absolutely impossible for him to ascertain—the intention of the priest. And not this alone. Before the priest, even with the best of intentions, has any power to consecrate the bread, and transform it into "the body and blood, soul and divinity" of the Lord, he must have been ordained by a bishop who should, at the time of ordaining, have had "the intention of doing what the Church does," and who in turn should have been ordained with a good intention by another bishop with a good intention, and so on *ad infinitum*, or at least *ad Petrum*. And when we bear in mind that the validity of the baptism of each of these depends just as absolutely on so many unknown and unknowable "intentions," and that in case of the invalidity of their baptism, which is "the gate of the sacraments," they were incapable of receiving ordination themselves, and so incapable of conferring it, the chance of Dr. Stone's ever getting a morsel of genuine, certainly attested "body and blood, soul and divinity" between his lips, becomes, to a mathematical mind, infinitesimal. There have been cases of ecclesiastics who in their death-bed confessions have acknowledged the withholding of multitudes of "intentions." Who can guess what multitudes besides have been withheld with never a confession, or with a confession which has never been heard of. But the wilful withholding need not be supposed. "The smallest mistake, even though made involuntarily, nullifies the whole act." *

---

* Pope Innocent III., Ep. ix. "The Council of Florence had pronounced the same opinion. . . . Let an infidel or a dreamy priest baptize a child without having seriously the idea of baptizing it, that child, if he die, is lost; let a bishop ordain a priest, without having actually and formally, from absence of mind or any other cause, the idea of conferring the priesthood, and behold, we have a priest who is not a priest, and those whom he shall baptize, marry or absolve, will not be baptized, married or absolved. The pope himself, without suspecting it, might have been ordained in this manner; and as it is from him that everything flows, all the bishops of the Church might some day find themselves to be false bishops, and all the priests false priests, without there being any possibility of restoring the broken link." Bungener, "Hist. of the Council of Trent," pp. 158, 159. The author evidently mistakes in making the validity of baptism to depend on priestly ordination. That alone of the sacraments is valid if administered (with intention) by a "Jew, pagan, or heretic."

Bungener need not have put the case hypothetically. Writing at the period of the Great Western Schism,

The hope of salvation through the sacraments of the Church grows dimmer and dimmer. It is well for our neophyte to cast about him and see if there be found no adjuvants that may reinforce in some measure that "assurance of his salvation," to which the Holy Father has somewhat inconsiderately invited him. "It is a good and useful thing," says the Council of Trent, "suppliantly to invoke the saints, and . . . to flee for refuge to their prayers, help and assistance." It is commonly represented to Protestants that this is a mere recommendation, and that nobody is required to invoke the saints; but Dr. Stone has by this time been long enough under discipline to have found out that this is nothing but a polite

"the papal secretary, Coluccio Salutato, paints in strong colors the universal uncertainty and anguish of conscience produced by the Schism, and his own conclusion as a Papalist is that as all ecclesiastical jurisdiction is derived from the pope, and as a pope invalidly elected cannot give what he does not himself possess, no bishops or priests ordained since the death of Gregory XI. could guarantee the validity of the sacraments they administered. It followed according to him, that any one who adored the Eucharist consecrated by a priest ordained in schism worshipped an idol. Such was the condition of Western Christendom."—The Pope and the Council, by Janus, p. 240.

It is doubtless, with reference to difficulties like these, that saving clauses are introduced into the utterances of the Church: "Without the sacraments or the desire for them;" "if any man wilfully separate from the communion of the Holy See," etc. But if these clauses save the difficulties of the Church's doctrine, then they destroy the doctrine itself. If the good intentions of the penitent are what secure to him the grace of the sacraments, then that grace does not depend on the intention of the priest; and the provision which so many souls are yearning for, of a through ticket to heaven that does not depend on their own interior character, is miserably cut off.

pretence, and to be convinced that if there is anything to be gained by saint-worship, he had better be about it, for "help and assistance" are what he is sadly in need of. But to which of the saints shall he take refuge? for there is an *embarras de richesses* here. As to some of them, there is a serious and painful uncertainty, as in the case of Mrs. Harris, as to whether there is "any such a person." As to others, there is a strong human probability that in the "unpleasantness" that prevailed between heathen and Christian in the early times, they were on the wrong side. And in general, the Church fails to give certain assurance, as *de fide*, concerning them, that they are yet in a position to act effectively as intercessors— whether, in fact, they are not to this day roasting in purgatory, and in sorer need of our intercession than we of theirs. The Church, we say, has not pronounced assuredly and *de fide* on this point; and what Dr. Stone is invited to by the Holy Father, and what doubtless he means to get, is assurance, not "pious opinion."

It will be "safer" for Dr. Stone "to seek salvation through the Virgin Mary" than directly from Jesus. So at least he is taught in books authorized and indorsed by the Church. But this is a very slender gain, for the same books assure him that without the intercession of Mary there is no safety at all—that "the intercession is not only useful but necessary"—that "to no one is the door of salvation open except through her"—that "our salvation is in her hands"—that "Mary is the hope of our salvation;"* so that the amount of this assurance (if one could be assured of its authority) is only this, that it is better than nothing at all.

Undoubtedly, the Rev. Dr. Stone would do well to get him a scapular. "About the year 1251, the Holy Virgin appeared to the blessed St. Simon Stock, an Englishman, and giving him her scapular, said to him that those who wore it should be safe from eternal damnation." Furthermore, "Mary appeared at another time to Pope John XXII., and directed him to declare to those who wore the above-mentioned scapular, that they should be released from pur-

---

* See "The Glories of Mary," by St. Alphonsus Liguori, approved by John, Archbishop of New York; chapter v., on "the need we have of the intercession of Mary for our salvation." It has been certified by the pope in the act of canonization that the writings of St. Alphonsus contain nothing worthy of censure. But as it is, up to this present writing, impossible to say certainly whether this was one of the pope's infallible utterances or one of his fallible ones—there we are again, in an uncertainty.

For a full collection of authorized Roman Catholic teachings, to the effect that "it is impossible for any to be saved who turn away from Mary, or is disregarded by her," see Pusey's Eirenicon. p. 99, seqq.—bearing in mind, however, the claim of the defenders of the Roman Catholic system, that their Church is not to be considered responsible for its own authorized teachings.

gatory on the Saturday after death"; this the same pontiff announced in his bull, which was afterwards confirmed by "several other popes."* This, declared in a book which is guaranteed by a pope to contain no false doctrine, is really the nearest that we can find in the entire Roman system to an assurance of salvation. But to the utter dismay of poor Dr. Stone, just as he is on the point of closing his hand on what the pope had invited him to—"laying hold," as an old writer expresses it, "on eternal life" in the form of a scapular—he discovers not only that Pope Paul V., in 1612, added a sort of codicil to the Virgin's promise, which makes it doubtful, but in general, that the inerrant author of the Glories of Mary "protests that he does not intend to attribute any other than purely human authority to all the miracles, revelations and incidents contained in this book."† But "purely human authority" is not exactly what we care to risk our everlasting salvation on; is it, Dr. Stone?

Nothing seems to remain for our bewildered friend but to apply for indulgences. To be sure, he does not yet know that he has ever been effectually loosed from

---
* Glories of Mary, pp 271, 272, 669.
† Glories of Mary, Protest of the Author, p. 1.

mortal sin, or if he has been, that he will not relapse into it and die in it; and in either case indulgences will do him no good. He will go down quick into hell, and not get his money back either. But, supposing him to have escaped eternal perdition, it will be well worth while to have secured indulgences—which may be had of assorted lengths, from twenty-five day indulgences for "naming reverently the name of Jesus, or the name of Mary," up to twenty-five thousand and thirty thousand year indulgences, granted for weightier considerations. But, inasmuch as Dr. Stone has not the slightest idea how many millions of years he may have to stay in purgatory, if he ever has the happiness to get there, it will be best for him to go in for plenary indulgences, and save all mistakes. There are various ways of securing them, and it may well employ all Dr. Stone's unquestionable talents how he shall get the amplest indulgence at the least cost of time and labor. On a superficial examination, we are disposed to think that there is nothing better to recommend than the wearing of scapulars.

Says St. Alphonsus de Liguori: "The indulgences that are attached to this scapular of our Lady of Mt. Carmel, as well as to the others of the Dolors of Mary, of Mary of Mercy, and particularly to that of the Conception, are innumerable, daily and plenary, in life and at the article of death. For myself, I have taken all the above scapulars. And let it be particularly made known that besides many particular indulgences, there are annexed to the scapular of the Immaculate Conception, which is blessed by the Theatine Fathers, all the indulgences which are granted to any religious order, pious place or person. And particularly by reciting 'Our Father,' 'Hail Mary,' and 'Glory be to the Father,' six times in honor of the most holy Trinity and of the immaculate Mary, are gained each time all the indulgences of Rome, Portiuncula, Jerusalem, Gallicia, which reach the number of four hundred and thirty-three plenary indulgences, besides the temporal, which are innumerable. All this is transcribed from a sheet printed by the same Theatine Fathers."* Oh, if the Theatine Fathers were only infallible, or if we could be sure that indulgences were absolute, and not conditional upon sundry uncertainties, how happy we might be. But a great theologian, afterwards a Pope,† declared that "the

---

*Glories of Mary, p. 661
† Pope Adrian VI., Comm. on the Fourth Book of The Sentences, quoted by Binzonur, Council of Trent, p 4

effects of the indulgence purchased or acquired, are not absolute, but more or less good, more or less complete, according to the dispositions of the penitent and the manner in which he performs the work to which the indulgence is attached." And one has only to glance through the pages of some theologian like Dr. Peter Dens, to find that this whole doctrine of indulgences is so contrived as to be, on the one hand, indefinitely corrupting and depraving to the common crowd of sinners, and, on the other hand, to give the least possible of solid comfort to fearful consciences. With every promise of remission that the Church gives—for a consideration —she reserves to herself a dozen qualifications and evasions which make it of none effect.*

In the dismal uncertainty which besets every expedient for securing one's salvation which we have thus far considered, our friend will devote himself in sheer desperation to works of mortification, which are

---

*Dens, Tractat. de Indulg., 34, 37, 38, 39, et passim. Says Cardinal Wiseman: "For you, my Catholic brethren, know that without a penitent confession of your sins and a worthy participation of the blessed Eucharist, no indulgence is anything worth." Doctrines of the Church. Vol. ii., p. 76. This, however, is said in a course of lectures designed to commend the doctrines of the Church to Protestants; when the object has been to comfort the devotee, or to raise revenue for the Roman treasury, the tone of the authorized representatives of the Church has sometimes been far more assuring.

alleged by his advisers to have a good tendency to "appease the wrath of God." Fastings and abstinences are good; but a hair shirt is far more effective, if his skin is tender; and we cannot doubt that flagellation is more serviceable than either. A good scourge is not expensive, but it should have bits of wire in the lashes, for a more rapid diminution of purgatorial pains. Sundry contrivances applied to one's bed, or to the sole of one's shoes, are recommended by the experience of some eminent saints as of great efficacy in securing one against future torment. It would not be well for Dr. Stone, in his quest for assurance, to omit any of them. But, alas! when he has done all, he is in the same dreary, dismal darkness as before.

Through such dim and doubtful ways the poor Doctor treads, halting and hesitating, till he comes towards the end of this weary life. Of all his friends who have departed this life before him, he has no confident assurance that they are not in hell; but he cherishes a hope that they may be roasting in the fires of purgatory, though he is aware that there is even a faint chance that they may be in heaven; but he pays for daily masses and indulgences in their behalf, being assured by the theologians that if these do not help his friends, they may in all probability be of service to some one else.* The nearest to certainty that he comes on any such question is in the belief that his godly parents and friends that have lived and died in simple faith on the Lord Jesus Christ, are suffering everlasting damnation—and even this is doubtful. As the hour of death draws near he feels for his various scapulars, and finds them right; he sends for his confessor, and makes one more confession, which is subject to all the doubtful conditions of those that have gone before; receives once more an absolution, which is absolute in its terms, but conditional in its meaning; and receives the half of a eucharist, the efficiency of which depends on an uncertain combination of conditions in his own soul and history, complicated with an utterly unascertainable series of facts in the hidden intention of every one of a series of priests and bishops back to Simon Peter himself. This done, the Church approaches him with a final sacrament, which promises once more to do what it thereby acknowledges that the other sacraments have failed to accomplish—to "wipe away offences, if any remain, and the remains of sin"—to "confer grace and remit sins."†

---

* Dens, Tract. de Indulg., No. 40.
† Conc. Trid. Sess. xiv., Can. 2.

But it is entirely unsettled among theologians what this promise means. It cannot be the remitting of mortal sin, for if the penitent have any such unforgiven, he is not allowed to receive the unction; and it cannot refer to venial sins, for a good many reasons that are laid down; and it cannot mean "proneness or habit left from past sin," for "it often happens that they who recover after the sacrament feel the same proneness to sin as before."* In fact, at the conclusion of the sacrament Dr. Stone will send for his lawyer, and if anything remains of his property after his heavy expenditure in masses and indulgences for the benefit of his deceased friends, he will leave it by will, to be given for masses to shorten up the torments which after all these labors and prayers to Mary, and mortifications, and sacraments, he still perceives to be inevitable † But, even in this he bethinks himself of the uncertainty whether masses, paid for in advance, will

---

* Bellarmine, de Extr. Unct. I., 9, T. ii., p. 1198, 9. Quoted in Pusey's Eirenicon, pp 211.

† A most striking instance of this is recorded in one of the most interesting and recent records of Roman Catholic piety—the Life of the Curé d'Ars. The old Curé of Ars had lived a life of preëminent holiness, in which his acts of self-mortification had been so austere and cruel as to have broken down his health—such that others could not hear them described without a shudder. As his death drew near he "desired to be fortified by the grace of the last sacrament"; and the Abbé Vianney

ever be actually said or sung.* But, poor soul, it is the best he can do, and so he gets them to give him a blessed taper to hold, and gives up the ghost while it burns out, and they sprinkle his body with holy water, and bury it in consecrated ground to keep it safe from the demons; and his children give their money to get him out of purgatory (in case he is there), and down to the latest generation never know (unless their money gives out) whether they have succeeded, or whether, in fact, he has not all the while been hopelessly in hell along with his good old father and mother.

We cannot better wind up this exhibition of the way in which the Church of Rome fulfils her promise of giving assurance of salvation, than by quoting the

---

then heard his confession, and administered to him the last rites of the Church. . . . "The following day the Abbé Vianney celebrated a mass for his revered master, at which all the villagers were present. When this service was concluded, M. Balley requested a private interview with his vicar. During this last and solemn conversation, the dying man placed in his hands the instruments of his penitence (scourges, etc.). 'Take care, my poor Vianney,' he said, 'to hide these things; if they find them after my death they will think I have done something during my life for the expiation of my sins, and they will leave me in purgatory to the end of the world.'" The Curé d'Ars. A Memoir of Jean-Baptiste-Marie Vianney. By Georgina Molyneux. London, 1869.

* There will hardly fail to occur to him the scandalous cause célèbre tried some years since in Paris— the case of a large brokerage in masses for the dead, which undertook to get the masses performed by country priests at a lower figure than the ruling city prices, but was detected in retaining the money without securing the saying of the masses at all.

language of a most competent witness, the Rev. J. Blanco White, once a Roman Catholic theologian in high standing in Spain, afterwards a Protestant, whose trustworthiness is vouched for by Father Newman, from intimate personal acquaintance.* Mr. White says:

"The Catholic who firmly believes in the absolving power of his Church, and never indulges in thought, easily allays all fears connected with the invisible world. Is there a priest at hand to bestow absolution at the last moment of life, he is sure of a place in heaven, however sharp the burnings may be which are appointed for him in purgatory.

"But, alas for the sensitive, the consistent, the delicate mind that takes the infallible church for its refuge! That church offers, indeed, certainty in everything that concerns our souls; but, Thou, God, who hast witnessed my misery and that of my nearest relations—my mother and my two sisters—knowest that the promised certainty is a bitter mockery. The Catholic pledges of spiritual safety re the most agonizing sources of doubt.

---

* "I have the fullest confidence in his word when he witnesses to facts, and facts which he knew." He was one "who had special means of knowing a Catholic country, and a man you can trust." Lectures on the Present Position of Catholics in England, by John Henry Newman, D.D. 1851.

"The sacraments intended for pardon of sins could not (according to the common notions) fail in producing the desired effect. For if, as was subsequently given out, all those divinely instituted rites demanded such a spiritual state in the recipient as, without any external addition, would produce the desired effect, what advantage would be offered to the believer? If absolution demanded true repentance to deliver from sin, this was leaving the sinner in the same condition as he was in before even the name of the pretended Sacrament of Penance was heard of in the world. But, if these conditions alone can give security, no thinking person, and especially no anxious, timid person, can find certainty in the use of the Sacraments. And none but the naturally bold and confident do find it. To these the Sacraments, instead of being means of virtue, are encouragements of vice and iniquity.

"O God! if Thou couldst hate anything Thou hast made, what weight of indignation would have fallen upon a Constantine and an Alva! And yet the former, having put off baptism till the last opportunity of sinning should be on the point of vanishing with the last breath of life, declares the heavenly happiness which filled his soul from the moment he came out of the baptismal water; the latter, that cold-blooded butcher of thousands, declares that he dies without the least remorse. On the other hand, have I not seen the most innocent among Thy worshippers live and die in a maddening fear of hell! They tremble at the Sacraments themselves, lest, from want of a firm preparation, they should increase their spiritual danger."*

It might be very tedious to read, but it would certainly be very easy to present, like proofs to show that in "heeding the invitation" of the Pope to come to him for infallible teaching in matters of *belief*, Dr. Stone has come only to like grief and anxious uncertainty. He has stated very neatly the fallacy of those who have sought for an infallible interpreter of scripture in the writings of the Fathers. "They do not see that in place of acting upon a new rule, they have only increased the difficulties of the old; that instead of obtaining an interpreter, they have only multiplied the number of the documents, which they must themselves interpret, or have interpreted for them"; and "are, in fact, re-

---

* Life of the Rev. Joseph Blanco White, written by himself. Edited by John Hamilton Thom. London, 1845. Vol. III., pp. 258-258.

sorting to what has been aptly called 'the most ingenious of all Protestant contrivances for submitting to nothing and nobody.'"* Marvellous! that a man who is so shrewd to perceive this fallacy in the system he has just left, should be so blind to the same fallacy in the system he has just adopted! He had

> "Jumped into a bramble bush
> And scratched out both his eyes;
>
> "And when he saw his eyes were out,
> With all his might and main,
> He jumped into another bush
> To scratch them in again."

By just so far as his new teacher is infallible, it is simply documentary—paper and printer's ink—Fathers, Councils, Bulls, Briefs, more Bulls, more Briefs, and another Council again, documents upon documents, all in the Latin tongue (which, happily, Dr. Stone is able to read), until the world cannot hold the books that have been written. But, on the other hand, just as far as he has access to his new teacher as a living teacher—a representative of the Catholic hierarchy—he finds him confessedly fallible—an uninspired priest or bishop, likely enough an unconvicted heretic, and at least liable to all human blunders and endless "varia-

---
* The Invitation Heeded, pp. 158, 159.

tions" in expounding and applying the faith of the Church. If, disgusted with these miserable comforters, he carries his doubts to the apostolic threshold, and receives a solution of them from the successor of Peter himself, it is a poor reward for his pilgrimage, when he learns that the words of the pontiff spoken in his capacity as a private teacher are no more infallible than those of any Protestant minister. So that the certainty of poor Dr. Stone's faith, unless he chooses the alternate risk of going to the documents himself, and taking his chance of being "saved by scholarship," or by "private interpretation," is resolved into the mere "fides implicita"—of being willing to believe the truth if he only knew what it was—and that, if we understand him, is just what he had before he got the Pope's letter, with the exception that at that time there were fewer elements of uncertainty in his mind.

And just as with questions of truth, so is it with questions of duty. In search of definiteness and certainty he has gone voyaging upon a waste of dreary casuistry, upon whose fluctuating surface he lies becalmed, tossed to and fro between "probabilism" and "probabiliorism," and oh, how seasick! There is nothing for him but to "do as they do in Spain"; and how that is we learn from Father Newman's friend, Blanco White:

"In a country where every person's conscience is in the keeping of another, in an interminable succession of moral trusts, the individual conscience cannot be under the steady discipline of self-governing principle; all that is practised is obedience to the opinion of others, and even that obedience is inseparably connected with the idea of a dispensing power. If you can obtain an opinion favorable to your wishes, the responsibility falls on the adviser, and you may enjoy yourself with safety. The adviser, on the other hand, having no consciousness of the action, has no sense of remorse; and thus the whole morality of the country, except in very peculiar cases, wants the steady ground of individual responsibility."*

The sum of the whole matter seems to be this, that the certainty and confidence of the disciple of the Church of Rome, whether regarding matter of belief or matter of practice, consists in putting his head in a bag and giving the string to his confessor.

The "invitation heeded" by Dr. Stone

---

* Life of J. Blanco White, I., p. 33.

contains other seductive promises, which it
would be well for us to consider if there
were time. We can only allude with a
word to the excellent things which His
Holiness offers, in this invitation, to society
and government in Protestant countries,
in pity of the misfortunes under which he
perceives them now to be suffering.

"Whoever recognizes religion as the
foundation of human society, cannot but
perceive and acknowledge what disastrous
effect this division of principles, this opposition, this strife of religious sects among
themselves, has had upon civil society, and
how powerfully this denial of the authority
established by God to determine the belief
of the human mind, and to direct the
actions of men as well in private as in
social life, has excited, spread, and fostered
those deplorable upheavals, those commotions by which almost all people are grievously disturbed and afflicted." "On this
longed-for return to the truth and unity
of the Catholic Church depends the salvation not only of individuals, but also of all
Christian society; and never can the world
enjoy true peace unless there shall be one
fold and one Shepherd."*

We see here the value of an infallible

---
* Letter of Pope Pius IX., Sept. 13, 1868.

teacher! If it had not been revealed to us thus from heaven, we never should have guessed that what secured national tranquillity was national adherence to the Holy See. But now we see it—by the eye of faith. Poor England, racked with intestine commotions!—if she could but learn the secret of Spanish order and tranquillity and prosperity! Unhappy Scotland, the prey of social anarchy, and devoured by thriftless indolence! will she not cast one glance across the sea, and lay to heart the lesson of Irish serenity and peace and wealth? Poor Protestant Prussia, and Denmark, and Scandinavia, "grievously disturbed and afflicted" by "those deplorable upheavals and commotions" which His Holiness talks about, and yet so pitifully unconscious of them all! How slight the price—a mere "Fall down and worship me"—with which they might purchase to themselves the sweet calmness and good order and unbroken quiet that have characterized the history of Catholic France and Italy, and even the ineffable beatitude of those happy States of the Church, which, ungrateful for their unparalleled blessings, were waiting at that very time for a good chance to put the Pope (in his temporal capacity) into the Tiber! Nay, nay! Let us not refuse to bring home the teaching of our Shepherd to our own bosoms. What land has been more the victim of "this division of principles, this opposition, this strife of religious sects among themselves," than our own unhappy country? Ah! were the people wise! Do they not feel the "disastrous effects" of their refusal to submit to the Holy See—the "deplorable upheavals, and commotions," and all? Can they resist the allurements of those examples of national happiness which fill the whole western hemisphere, save the two pitiable exceptions of Canada and the United States? Speak, dear Dr. Stone, speak once more to your infatuated fellow-countrymen, and persuade them, if you can, to end this hundred years' history of commotion and revolution and disastrous change which they have lately completed, by substituting the majestic stability of Mexico, and Guatemala, and Colombia, and all the Catholic continent down to the Straits of Magellan![*] Al-

---

[*] Father Hyacinthe does not seem to come up to the standard of Roman doctrine on this point. "Ah, well, I know—and n any a time have I groaned within myself to think of it—these nations of the Latin race and of the Catholic religion have been of late the most grievously tried of all! Not only by intestine fires, by the quaking of the earth, by the inrushing of the sea. Look with impartial eye, with the fearless serenity of truth, with that assurance of faith which fears not to accept the revelations of experience, and then tell me where it is that the moral foundations quake most violently? Where

ready a ray of hope shines in upon the darkness of the Protestant land. One bright spot is irradiated with the triumph—the partial triumph—of Roman principles of government. Can it be irrational to hope that when these principles prevail in the same degree throughout the land, we shall have everywhere, under state and general governments, the same placid order, the same security for life and property, the same freedom from turbulence and riot, the same purity of elections, the same integrity in the discharge of public trusts, the same awfulness of judicial virtue as prevail in the Catholic city and county of New York?

We have left ourselves very little space to express as we would like the real respect which, after all, we feel for this book, and still more for its author. With here and there a slip in grammar or diction, and with no more of pedantry than can easily be pardoned to the author's vocation, the work is elegantly written; and if there does seem to be a dreadful gap between

does the current of a formidable electricity give the severest, the most incessant shocks to republics as well as monarchies? Among the Latin races, among the Catholic nations. Yes, by some inscrutable design of Providence, they, more than others, have had to 'drink of the cup deep and large'; they have wet their lips more deeply in the chalice in which are mingled 'the wine, the lightning, and the spirit of the storm'; and they have become possessed with the madness of the drunkard." Discourses of Father Hyacinthe, Vol. I., p. 155.

what the author intended when he started,
and what he found where he stopped, it
must be acknowledged that he passes from
starting point to goal with consecutive steps
along an intelligible path. His argument,
although encumbered with mistakes, is,
nevertheless, good against any opponent
who accepts his premise—that the Church
Universal is a visible corporation. His
appeal to all Protestants to examine with
candor the grounds of their belief, and
bravely and sincerely accept the consequences,
is earnest, tender and touching—
all the more so, as the unhappy author in
his very exhortation, evidently looks back
upon those generous moments when he
himself was practising these virtues, as
Adam might have looked back upon Paradise.
Those hours can never return. Never
more may he exercise the manly virtue
which he now commends to others, and
which we doubt not he faithfully practised
until it became a prohibited good. Let
him now attempt to look into the writings
of those who differ from him, with a view
to "examining candidly the grounds of his
faith," and the thunderbolt of the excommunication *lata sententia* breaks forth
upon him from the Bull *In Cœna Domini*.*

---

* Ligori Theol Moral. 63, 735.

We are so affected by the honest doctor's exhortation to candid inquiry, that we shrink from putting ourselves, like him, in a situation in which if we candidly inquire we are damned.

The little volume will reasonably be expected to be more effective as a fact and a testimony than as an argument. As a testimony, its precise value is this: Until middle life, the author, believing himself to be entirely sincere and candid, held, as the result of private judgment, a system (according to his own statement) wildly inconsistent, illogical and self-destructive, which he vindicated to himself and others by arguments plausible and satisfactory. In the course of a few months, after candid but brief examination, in the exercise of the same private judgment, he dropped that system and (also with entire sincerity) adopted another, sustained by plausible arguments which he is not permitted candidly to re-examine. It is solely by the use of the same private judgment that played him so false before, that he has come to embrace this other system.

Qu.:—What is the probability that he has got the truth now?

That is what he may never know.

One thing alone he holds intelligently—

that the Roman Church is the true church of Christ; and this he knows only by his poor private judgment, which he is not permitted to revise. Everything else he takes on the authority of this. And this, being known only by private judgment, may be a mistake!

Poor man!

THE REAL PRISONER OF CHILLON

THE REAL PRISONER
OF CHILLON.

"A CHARACTER more celebrated than known" is Francis Bonivard, prior of St. Victor and Prisoner of Chillon. It is not by any intentional imposture on his part that he goes stalking through modern literature disguised in the character of hero, saint and martyr, and shouting in a hoarse chest-voice his "appeal from tyranny to God." In fact, if he could be permitted to revisit his cherished little shelf of books about which has grown the ample library of the University of Geneva, and view the various delineations of himself by artist, poet, and even serious historian, it would be delightful to witness his comical astonishment. Perhaps it is not to be laid to the fault of Lord Byron, who after visiting the old castle and its dungeon beguiled the hours of a rainy day at the inn at Ouchy with writing a poem concerning which he frankly confesses that he had not the slightest knowledge of its hero. Hobhouse, his companion, ought to have been better informed, but was not. If anybody is to blame, it is the recent writers, who do know the facts, but are unwilling to hurt so fine an heroic figure or to dethrone "one of the demigods of the liberal mythology." Enough to say that the Muse of History has been guilty of one of those practical jokes to which she is too much addicted, in dressing with tragic buskins and muffling in the cloak of a hero of melodrama, and so palming off for earnest on two generations of mankind, the drollest wag of the sixteenth century.

A wild young fellow like Bonivard, with a lively appreciation of the ridiculous, could not fail to see the comic aspect of the fate which invested him with the spiritual and temporal authority and emoluments of the priory of St. Victor. This was a rich little Benedictine monastery just outside the eastern gate of Geneva, on the little knoll now crowned by the observatory, surrounded with walls and moat of its own, independent of the Bishop of Geneva in spiritual matters, and in temporal affairs equally independent of the city: in fact, it was a petty sovereignty by itself, and its dozen of hearty, well-provided monks, though nominally under the rule of Cluny, were a law to themselves, and not a very rigid one either. The office of prior, by virtue of a little arrangement at Rome, descended to Bonivard from his uncle, immediately upon whose demise the young potentate of twenty-one took upon him the state and functions of his office in a way to show the monks of St. Victor that they had no King Log to deal with. The document is still extant in the Latin of the period, in which Prior Bonivard ordains that every new brother at his initiation shall not only stand treat all round, but shall, at his own cost and charges, furnish every one of his brethren with a new cap. Another document of equal gravity makes new ordinances concerning the convent-kitchen, which seems to have been one of the good prior's most religious cares.* Not only his own subjects, but those of other jurisdictions, were made to feel the majesty of his sovereign authority. He would let them know that he had "just as much jurisdiction at St. Victor as the Duke of Savoy had at Chambéry." He heard causes, sentenced to prison, even received ambassadors from his brother the duke, but not without looking sharply at their credentials. If these were wanting, the unfortunate wretches were threatened with the gallows

---

* The documents are given in full in the appendix of Dr. J. J. Chapponière's memoir in vol. iv. of the *Mém. de la Soc. Archæol. de Genève*. The former is signed by Bonivard, apostolic prothonotary and *poet-laureate*.

as spies, and when they had been thoroughly frightened the monarch would indulge himself in the exercise of the sweetest prerogative of royalty, the pardoning power, and, when it was considered that the majesty of the state had been sufficiently asserted, would wind up with asking the whole company to dinner.

It had been considered a clever stroke of policy, at a time when the dukes of Savoy and the bishops of Geneva, who agreed in nothing else, were plotting, together or separately, to capture and extinguish the immemorial liberties of the brave little free city, to get this fortified outpost before its very gate officered by a brilliant and daring young Savoyard gentleman, who would be bound to the duke by his nativity and to the Church by his office, and to both by his interests. To the dismay of bishop and duke, it appeared that the young prior, who had led a gay life of it at the University of Turin, had nevertheless read his classics to some purpose, and had come back with his head full of Plato and Plutarch and Livy and of theories of republican liberty. So that by putting him into St. Victor they had turned that little stronghold from an outpost of attack upon Geneva liberties into the favorite resort and rendezvous of all the young liberal leaders of that gay but gallant little republic, who found themselves irresistibly drawn to young Bonivard, partly as a republican and still more as a jolly good fellow.

The first manifestation of his sympathies in that direction occurred soon after his installation as prior. His uncle on his deathbed had confessed to young Francis the burden on his conscience in that he had taken Church money and applied it to the making of a battery of culverins wherewith to levy war against one of his neighbors in the country; and bequeathed to his nephew the convent and the culverins, with the charge to melt down the latter into a chime of church-bells which should atone for his evil deeds. Not long after, Bonivard was telling the story to his friend, Berthelier, the daring and heroic leader of the "Sons of Geneva" in their perilous struggle against tyranny, when the latter exclaimed: "What! spoil good cannon to make bells? Never! Give us the guns, and you shall have old metal to make bells enough to split your ears. But let guns be guns. So the Church will be doubly served. There will be chimes at St. Victor and guns in Geneva, which is a Church city." The bargain was struck, as a vote in the records of the city council shows to this day. But it was the beginning of a quarrel with the Duke of Savoy which was to cost Bonivard more than he had counted on. There was reckless deviltry enough among all these young liberals, but some of them—not Bonivard—were capable of seriously counting the cost of their game. On one occasion —it was at the christening of Berthelier's child, and Bonivard was godfather—Berthelier took his friend aside from the guests and said, "It is time we had done with dancing and junketing and organized for the defence of liberty."—"All right!" said the prior. "Come on, and may the Lord prosper our crazy schemes!" Berthelier took his hand, and with a serious look that sobered the rattle-headed ecclesiastic for a moment, replied, "But let me warn you that this is going to cost you your living and me my head."—"I have heard him say this a hundred times," says Bonivard in his *Chronicles*. The dungeon at Chillon and the mural tablet in the Tour de l'Isle at Geneva tell how truly the prophecy was fulfilled.

There was so little of the strut of the stage-hero about Bonivard that he could not be comfortable in doing a chivalrous thing without a joke to take off the gloss of it. Before the ducal party had quite given up hopes of him there was a serious affair on their hands—the need of putting out of the way by such means, treacherous and atrocious, as the Savoyards of that day loved to use, one of the noblest of the Geneva magistrates, Aimé Lévrier. An emissary of the duke, of high rank, kinsman to Bonivard, came to St. Victor and offered the prior magnificent inducements to aid in the plot. With a gravity that must have convulsed the spectators if there had been any, Bonivard pointed to his monastic gown, his prayer-book and his crucifix, and pleaded his deep sense of the sacredness of his office as a reason for having nothing to do with the affair. "Then," says his kinsman, rising in wrath, "I will do the business myself. I'll have Lévrier out of his bed and over in Savoy this very night."—"Do you really mean it, uncle? Give me your hand!"—"Then you consent, after all, to help me in the matter?"—"Oh no, uncle, that isn't it. But I know these Genevese are a hasty sort of folk, and I am just going to raise thirty florins to be spent in saying masses to-morrow for the repose of your soul." Before the evening was over, Bonivard found an opportunity of slipping in disguise over to the house of Lévrier and giving a hint of what was intended: the notes of preparation for resistance that Berthelier and his friends began at once to make wrought upon the excited nerves of the ambassador and his armed retinue to such a point that they were fain to escape from the town by a secret gate before daylight.

The affair of his rescue of Pécolat is another illustration of his character and of the strange, turbulent age in which he lived; and it went far to embitter the hatred of the duke and the bishop against him. This poor fellow was the jester, song-singer and epigrammatist of the madcap patriots who were associated under the title of "Sons of Geneva." Under a trumped-up charge of plotting the death of the bishop he was kidnapped and carried away to one of the castles in the neighborhood, and there tortured until a false confession was wrung from him implicating Berthelier and others. To secure his condemnation to death he was brought back into the city and presented before the court; but the sight of the poor cripple, racked and bruised with recent tortures, and his steadfastness in recanting his late confession, wrought more with the judges than

the fear of the duke, and he was acquitted.
But the feeble and ferocious bishop, moved
partly by malignity, and partly, no doubt,
by sincere and cowardly terror, was resolved to kill him; and by some fiction declaring him to have been in the minor
orders, he clapped him into the bishop's
prison, claiming to try him by ecclesiastical
law. The story of renewed tortures inflicted on their helpless comrade, and their
knowledge of the certain death that awaited
him, stirred the blood of the patriots of
Geneva. It was just the moment for the
prior of St. Victor to show that the studies
at Freiburg and Turin that had made him
doctor utriusque juris had not been in
vain. He would fight the bishop with his
own weapon of Church law. He despatched
Pécolat's own brother with letters to the
Archbishop of Vienne, metropolitan to the
Bishop of Geneva, and, using his family influence, which was not small, he secured a
summons to the bishop and chapter of
Geneva to appear before the archiepiscopal
court and give account of the affair, and
meanwhile to cease all proceedings against
the prisoner.

It was comparatively easy to procure the
summons. The difficulty was to find some
one competent to the functions of episcopal

usher and bold enough to serve it. Bonivard bethought him of a "caitiff wretch" —an obscure priest—to whom he handed the document with two round dollars lying on it, and bade him hand the paper to the bishop at mass the next day in the cathedral. The starving clergyman hesitated long between his fears and his necessities, but finally promised to do the work on condition that the prior should stand by him in person and see him through. The hour approached, and the commissioner's courage was oozing rapidly away. His knees knocked together, and he slipped back in the crowd, hoping to escape. The vigilant prior darted after him, seized him, and laying his hand on the dagger that he wore under his robe, whispered in his ear, " Do it or I'll stab you !" He adds, in his *Chronicles*, "I should have been as good as my word : I do not say it by way of boasting. I know I was acting like a fool, but I was quite beside myself with anxiety for my friend." Happily, there was no need of extreme measures. He gripped his terrified victim by the thumb, and as the procession moved towards the church-door he thrust the paper into his hand, saying, "Now's the time ! You've got to do it." And all the time he held him fast by the thumb. The bishop came near, and Bonivard let go the wretch's thumb and pushed him to the front, pointing to the prelate and saying, "Do your work!" The bishop turned pale with terror of assassination as he heard the words. But the trembling clerk, not less terrified than the bishop, dropped on his knees and presented the archiepiscopal mandate, gasping out, "My lord, *inhibitur vobis, prout in copia.*" Bonivard retreated into his inviolable sanctuary of St. Victor. "I was young enough and crazy enough," he says, "to fear neither bishop nor duke." He had saved poor Pécolat's life, although the work was not finished until the publication of an interdict from the metropolitan silencing every church-bell and extinguishing every altar-candle in the city had brought the bishop to terms.[*]

It is a hardship to the writer to be compelled to retrench the story of the early deeds for liberty of Bonivard and his boon companions. There is a rollicking swagger about them all, which by and by begins to be sobered when it is seen that "on the side of the oppressor there is *power.*" By violence,

---

[*] The story is told by Bonivard himself in his *Chronicles*, and may be found in full detail in the Second Series of Dr. Merle d'Aubigné's volumes on the Reformation, vol. i. chaps. viii. and x. The story that Pécolat, about to be submitted a second time to the torture, and fearing lest he might be again tempted to accuse his friends, attempted to cut off his own tongue with a razor, seems to be authenticated. The whole story is worthy of being told at full length in English, it is so full of generous heroism.

by fraudulent promises, by foul treachery on the part of cowardly citizens, the Duke of Savoy gains admittance with his army within the walls of Geneva, and begins his delicious and bloody revenge for the indignities that have been put upon his pretensions and usurpations. Berthelier, a very copy from the antique—a hero that might have stepped forth into the sixteenth century from the page of Plutarch *—remained in the town serenely to await the death which he foreknew. On the day of the duke's entrance Bonivard, who had no such relish for martyrdom for its own sake, put himself between two of his most trusted friends, the Lord of Voruz and the Abbot of Montheron of the Pays de Vaud, and galloped away disguised as a monk. "Come first to my convent," said the abbot, "and thence we will take you to a place of safety." The convent was reached, and in the morning Bonivard was greeted by his comrade Voruz, who came into his room, and, laying paper and pen before him, required him to write a renunciation of his priory in favor of the Abbot of Montheron. Resistance was vain. He was a prisoner in the hands of traitors. The alternative being

---

* "Je n'ai vu ni lu oncques un si grand mépriseur de mort," says Bonivard in his *Chronicles*.

"Your priory or your life!" he frankly owns that he required no time at all to make up his choice. Voruz took the precious document, with the signature still wet, and went out, double locking the door behind him. His two friends turned him over to the custody of the duke, who locked him up for two years at Grolée, one of his castles down the Rhone, and put the honest Abbot of Montheron in possession of the rich living of St. Victor.

But Bonivard in his prison was less to be pitied than the citizens of Geneva who remained in their subjugated city. The two despots, the bishop and the duke, who had seized the unhappy town, combined to crush the gay and insubordinate spirit out of it. All this time, says Bonivard, "they imprisoned, they scourged, they tortured, they beheaded, they hung, so as it is pitiful to tell."

Meanwhile, the influential family friends of Bonivard, some of them high in court favor, discovering that he was yet alive and in prison, bestirred themselves to procure his liberation; and not in vain, for the possession that had made him dangerous, the priory of St. Victor, having been wrested from him, there was little harm that he could do. His immediate successor in the priory, good Abbot de Montheron, had not indeed long enjoyed the benefice. He had gone on business to Rome, where certain Churchmen who admired his new benefice invited him (so Bonivard tells the story) to a banquet *more Romano,* and gave him a dose of the "cardinal powder," which operated so powerfully that it purged the soul right out of the body. He left a paper behind him in which, as a sign of remorse for his crime, he resigned all his rights in the priory back to Bonivard.* But the pope, whose natural affection towards his cousins and nephews overflowed freely in the form of gifts of what did not belong to him, bestowed the living on a cousin, who commuted it for an annual revenue of six hundred and forty gold crowns—a splendid revenue for those days—and poor Bonivard, whose sole avocation was that of gentleman, found it difficult to carry on this line of business with neither capital nor income. He came back, some five years later, into possession of the priory. They were five years of exciting changes, of fierce terrorism and oppression at Geneva, followed by a respite, a rallying of the spirit of the people, an actual recovery of some of the old rights of the city, and,

---

* The text of this act is given by Chaponnière, p. 156.

presently, by the beginning of some signs of religious light coming from the direction of Germany. And the way in which Bonivard at last got reinstalled into his convent is curiously illustrative of the strange condition of society in those times. One May morning in 1527 the little town was all agog with strange news from Rome. The Eternal City had been taken by storm, sacked, pillaged, burned! The Roman bishop was prisoner to the Roman emperor, if indeed he was alive at all. In fact, there was a rumor—dreadful, no doubt, but attended by vast consolations—that the whole court of Rome had perished. Immediately there was a rush to the bishop's palace, and a scramble for the vacant livings in the diocese that had been held by absentees at Rome. The bishop, delighted at such a windfall of patronage, dispensed his favors right and left, not forgetting, says Bonivard, to reserve something comfortable for himself in the shape of a fat convent that had been held by a cardinal. This was Bonivard's opportunity, and, times and the bishop having changed, he got back once more into his cherished quarters as prior of St. Victor. The convent was there, and the friars, but the estates that had been wont to keep them all right royally were mostly in the hands of the duke and his minions. It is in the effort to recover these that Bonivard shines out in his most magnificent character, that of military hero. The campaign of Cartigny includes the most memorable of his feats of arms.

Cartigny was an estate about six miles down the left bank of the Rhone from Geneva appertaining to St. Victor. "It was a chastel of pleasaunce, not a forteresse," says our hero, who is the Homer of his own brave deeds. But the duke kept a garrison there, and to every demand the prior made for his place he replied that he did not dare give it up for fear of being excommunicated by the pope. Rent-time came, and the Savoyard Government enjoined the tenants not to pay to the prior. Whereupon that potentate declared that, being refused civil justice, he "fell back on the law of nations."

The military resources of his realm were limited. He counted ten able-bodied subjects, but they were monks and not liable to service. The culverins of his uncle were gone, but he had six muskets—a loan from the city—and there were four pounds of powder in the magazine. But this was not of itself sufficient for a war against the

Duke of Savoy. He must subsidize mercenaries.

About this time there chanced to be at Geneva a swashbuckler from Berne, Bischelbach by name, by trade a butcher, who had found the new régime of the Reformers at that city too straitlaced for his tastes and habits, and had come to Geneva, with some vagabonds at his heels, in search of adventures and a livelihood. Him did the prior of St. Victor, greatly impressed with his own accounts of his powers, commission as generalissimo of the forces. Second in command he set a priest, likewise just thrown out of business by the Reformation in the North ; and in a council of war the plan of campaign was determined. But before the actual clash of arms began, the solemn preliminaries usual between hostile powers must be scrupulously fulfilled. A herald was commissioned to make proclamation in the name of the lord of St. Victor, through all the lands of Cartigny, that no man should venture to execute there any orders, whether of pope or duke, under penalty of being hung. This energetic procedure struck due terror, for when Bonivard's captain with several soldiers appeared before the castle it capitulated without a blow.

It was a brief though splendid victory. The very first raid in which the "Knights of the Spoon"—an association of neighboring country gentlemen—harried that region they found that the capitain and entire garrison of the castle had gone to market (not without imputations of treason), leaving the post in charge of one woman, who promptly surrendered.

The sovereign of St. Victor's blood was up. He resolved to draw, if need were, on the entire resources of his realm. The army was promptly reinforced to twenty men, and Bonivard took the field in person at the head of his forces. On what wise this array debouched in two corps d'armée one Sunday morning from two of the gates of Geneva; how the junction of the forces was effected; the military history of the march; how they appeared, at last, before the castle of Cartigny—are these not written by the pen of the hero himself in his *Chronicles* of Geneva? But Bonivard, though brave, was merciful. Willing to spare the effusion of blood, he sent the general-in-chief, Bischelbach, with his servant Diebolt as an interpreter, to summon the castle. The answer was a shot that knocked poor Diebolt over with a mortal wound; whereupon the attacking army fell back in a masterly manner into the woods and made good their way into Geneva, bringing one prisoner, whom they had caught unarmed near the castle, and leaving Diebolt to die at a roadside inn.

We may not further narrate the deeds of Bonivard as a martial hero, though they are neither few nor uninteresting.* But he is equally worthy of himself as a religious reformer. It was about this time that the stirrings of religious reformation at Berne and elsewhere began to be heard at Geneva, and the thought began to be seriously entertained by some of the patriotic "Sons of Geneva" that perhaps that liberty for which they had dared and suffered so much in vain might best come with that gospel which had wrought such wonders in other communities. There was one man who could advise them what to do; and they went together over to the convent and sought audience and ghostly counsel of the

---

* We have the history of one of them in a brief of Pope Clement VII. addressed to the chapter and senate of Geneva, in which he expresses his sorrow that in a city which he has carried in his bowels so long such highhanded doings should be allowed. One Francis Bonivard has not only despoiled the rightful prior of his living, but —what is worse—has chased his attorney with a gun and shot the horse that he was running away upon: "*quodque pejus est, Franciscum Tingum ejusdem electi procuratorem, negocium restitucionis dictæ possessionis prosequentem, scloppettis invasisse, et equum super quo fugiebat vulnerasse.*" His Holiness threatens spiritual vengeance, and explains his zeal in the case by the fact that the excluded prior is his cousin.

prior. "We are going to have done with all popish ceremonies," said they, "and drive out the whole rabble-rout of papistry, monks, priests, and all: then we mean to send for gospel ministers to introduce the true Christian Reformation." It is pleasant to imagine the expression of Bonivard's countenance as he replied to his ardent friends: "It is a very praiseworthy idea. There is no doubt that all these ecclesiastics sadly need reformation. I am one of them myself. But who is to do the reforming? Whoever it is, they had better begin operations on themselves. If you are so fond of the gospel, why don't you practise it? It looks as if you did not so much love the gospel as you hate us. And what do you hate us for? It is not because we are so different from you, but because we are so like. You say we are a licentious lot; well, so are you. We drink hard; so do you. We gamble and we swear; but what do you do, I should like to know? Why should you be so hard on us? We don't interfere with your little enjoyments: for pity's sake, don't meddle with ours. You talk about driving us out and sending for the Lutheran ministers. Gentlemen, think twice before you do it. They will not have been here two years before you will wish they were gone. If you dislike us because we are too much like you, you will detest them because they are so different from you. My friends, do one thing or the other. Either let us alone, or, if you must do some reforming, try it on yourselves."

Thus did this excellent pastor, in the spirit of the gospel injunction to count the cost, give spiritual counsel to those who sought reformation of the Church. "I warrant you," he wrote concerning them, "they went off with their tails between their legs. I am as fond of reformation as anybody, but I am a little scrupulous as to who shall take it in hand." *

Bonivard's harum-scarum raids into the Duke of Savoy's dominions after rents or reprisals at last became so embarrassing to his Geneva friends that, much as they enjoyed the fun of them, it became necessary to say to the good monk that this sort of thing really must stop; and feeling the force of his argument, that he must have *something* to live on, the city council allowed its neighboring potentate a subvention of four crowns and a half monthly to enable him to keep up a state worthy of the dignity of a sovereign. He grumbled at the amount, but took it; and thereafter

* *Advis et Devis des difformes Reformateurs*, pp. 140–151.

the peace of Europe was less disturbed on his part.

But bad news came to the gay prior in his impoverished monastery. His mother was ill at his old home at Seyssel in Savoy, and he must see her before she died. It was venturing into the tiger's den, as all his friends told him, and as he did not need to be told. But he thought he would adventure it if he could get a safe-conduct from the tiger. The matter was arranged: the duke sent Bonivard his passport, limited to a single month; and the prior arrived at Seyssel, and nearly frightened the poor old lady out of her last breath with her sense of the peril to which he had exposed himself.

Our hero's incomparable genius for getting himself into difficulties never shone more brightly than at this hour. While here in the country of his mortal enemy, on the last days of his expiring safe-conduct, he got news of accusations gravely sustained at Geneva that he had gone over into Savoy to treat with the enemy. He did not dare to stay: he did not dare to go back. If he could get his safe-conduct extended for one month, to the end of May, he would try to make his way through the Pays de Vaud (then belonging to Savoy) to Fribourg in the Swiss Confederation. The extension was granted, and with many assurances of good-will from friends of the duke he pushed on. It was a fine May morning, the 26th, that he was on his last day's journey to Lausanne, and passing through a pine wood. Suddenly men sprang from ambush upon Bonivard, who grasped his sword and spurred, calling to his guide, "Put spurs!" But instead of so doing the guide turned and whipped out his knife and cut Bonivard's sword-belt; "Whereupon these worthy gentlemen," says Bonivard's *Chronicle*, "jumped on me and took me prisoner in the name of my lord duke." Safe-conducts were in vain. A bagful of ropes was produced, and he was carried on a mule, bound hand and foot, in secrecy, to the duke's castle of Chillon, the captain of which was one of the ambuscading party. For six years he was hidden from the world, and at first men knew not whether he was alive or dead. But his sufferings at the hand of the common foe put to shame the suspicions that had been engendered at Geneva, and it is recorded, to the honor of the Genevese, that during all that period, whenever negotiations were opened between them and the Duke of Savoy, the liberation of

Bonivard was always insisted on as one of the conditions.

The story of the imprisonment is soon told; for, strangely enough, this most garrulously egotistical of writers never alludes to it but twice, and then briefly. The first two years he was kept in the upper chambers of the castle and treated kindly, but at the end of this time the castle received a visit from the duke, and from that time forth the Prisoner of Chillon was remanded to the awful and sombre crypt. A single sentence in his handwriting is all that he tells us of this period, of which he might have told so much, and in this he shows a disposition to look at the affair rather in its humorous than its Byronesque aspect. For his one recorded reminiscence of his four years of dungeon-life is, that "he had such abundant leisure for promenading that he wore in the rock pavement a little path as neatly as if it had been done with a stone-hammer."*

---

* It is needful to caution enthusiastic tourists that nearly all the details of Byron's poem are fabulous. The two brothers, the martyred father, the anguish of the prisoner, were all invented by the poet on that rainy day in the tavern at Ouchy. Even the level of the dungeon, below the water of the lake, turns out to be a mistake, although Bonivard believed it: the floor of the crypt is eight feet above high-water mark. As for the thoughts of the prisoner, they seem to have been mainly occupied with making Latin and French verses of an objectionable sort not adapted for general publication. (See Ls. Vulliemin: *Chillon, Étude historique*, Lausanne, 1851.)

One March morning in 1536 the Prisoner of Chillon heard through the windows of his dungeon the sound of a cannonade by land and lake. It was the army of Berne, which was finishing its victorious campaign through the Pays de Vaud by the siege of the duke's last remaining stronghold, the castle of Chillon. They were joyfully aided by a flotilla fitted out by Geneva, which had never forgotten its old friend. That night the dungeon-door was burst open, and Bonivard and three fellow-prisoners were carried off in triumph to Geneva.

Not Rip Van Winkle when he awoke from his long slumber in the Catskills, not the Seven Sleepers of Ephesus when they came back from their sepulchre and found their city Christian, had a better right to be surprised than the prior of St. Victor when he got back to Geneva. Duke and bishop and all their functionaries were expelled; priests and preaching-friars were gone; the mass was abolished; in the cathedral of St. Peter's and all the lesser churches, which had been cleared of their images, there were singing of psalms and preaching of fiery sermons by Reformers from France; and the streets through which he had sometimes had to move by stealth were filled with joyous crowds to hail him as a martyr. St. Victor was no more. If he went to look for his old home, he found a heap of rubbish, for all the suburbs of the city that might give shelter to an enemy had been torn down by the unsparing patriots of Geneva, and the trees had been felled. The joyous city had ceased, and Bonivard's prophecy to his roystering companions was not long in being fulfilled for himself as well as for them: they soon found Calvin's little finger to be heavier than the bishop's loins.

And yet the heroic little town showed a noble gratitude towards the old friend of its liberties. The house which he chose out of all the city was given him for his own and furnished at the public expense. A pension of two hundred crowns a year in gold was settled on him, and he was made a senator of the republic. To all which was added a condition that he should lead a respectable life—a proviso which is practically explained in the very next appearance of his name in the records on account of a misdemeanor for which his accomplice was ordered to quit the town within three days.

The more generous was the town the more exacting became the Martyr. He could not get over his free-and-easy way

of living in the gay old days when the
tithes of his benefice yielded him nigh a
thousand yellow crowns a year. He could
not see why he was not entitled to have
his rents back again; and after a vain effort on the part of the council to make him
see it, he went off to Berne, where he had
been admitted a citizen, to ask it to interfere for him, sending back an impudent
letter renouncing his Geneva citizenship,
on the ground that in his reduced circumstances he could not afford to be a citizen
in two places at once. For a while the
patient city lost its patience with its unruly
beneficiary, but the genuine grateful and
kindly feeling that every one felt for the
poor fellow, and the general admiration for
his learning and wit, conspired with his
growing embarrassments to bring about a
settlement of the affair on the basis of a
reduced pension with a round lump sum to
pay his debts.

They sent for him two or three years
later to come to Geneva as historiographer,
and he came, bringing with him a wife from
Berne, who died soon after his arrival.
For a man of his years, he had a remarkable alacrity at getting married, and his
second venture was an unlucky one. For
from the wedding-day onward, when he

was not before the council with some quarrel or some affair of debt, he was apt to come before it to get them to compel his wife to live with him, or, failing that, to get her money to live on himself. What time could be saved from these wranglings, which lasted almost till the poor woman's death, was devoted ardently to his literary work. The history grew apace, and other books besides. In the seditions of the Libertine party against the austerities of the new régime the old man took the side of law and order and good morals in his book on *L'ancienne et nouvelle Police de Genève,* with an ardor that was the more surprising as one remembered his antecedents. In the midst of his toils he found time to get married to a third wife and to go to law with his neighbors. He is continually coming to the council, sometimes for a little loan to help him with his lawsuits, sometimes for relief in his embarrassments. It is touching to see how tender they are towards the poor foolish old man. They make him little grants from time to time, always looking to it that their money shall be applied to the object designated, and not "on his fantasies." They take up one of his notes for him, looking to see that it has not been tampered with because "he is easily circumvented and not adroit in his business." He complains of the heat during an illness one summer, and the seigneurie give him the White Chamber in the town-hall, and when winter comes on and he is old, and infirm, they assign him the lodging lately occupied by Mathurin Cordier (famous schoolmaster Corderius, whose *Dialogues* were the first book in Latin of our grandfathers), because it contained a stove—a rare luxury. He thanks them for their kindness as his fathers, and makes them heirs of his library and manuscripts.

There was another and more solemn assemblage, his relations with which were less tender. This was the consistory of the Church, which found it less easy to allow for the old man's infirmities. His first appearance before this body was under accusation of playing at dice with Clement Marot, another famous character and the sweet singer of the French Reformation. He comes next time of his own accord, asking the venerable brethren to interfere because his second wife ran away from him on their wedding-day, she defending herself on the ground of a bad cold. His domestic troubles bring him hither so often as to put the clergy out of patience. He is called up for beating his wife, but shows that the discipline was needed, and she is admonished to be more obedient in future. Later on he is questioned why he does not come to church. He can't walk, is the answer. But he is told that if he can get himself carried to the hôtel de ville to see the new carvings, he could get carried to church. And why does he neglect the communion? *Answer:* He has been debarred from it. "Then present your request to be restored." So the poor old gentleman presents himself six weeks later, asking to be readmitted to the Church; which is granted, but with the remark, entered on the record, that he "does not show much contrition in coming with a bunch of flowers over his ear—a thing very unbecoming in a man of his years."

The dreadful consistory had a principal concern in the affair that darkened the declining days of Bonivard with the shadow of a tragedy. An escaped nun had found refuge in his lodgings after his third wife's death; and after some love-making—on which side was disputed—there was a promise of marriage given by him, which, however, he was in no hurry to fulfil. The consistory deemed it best to interfere, in the interests of propriety, and insist on the marriage; and the decrepit old invalid in vain pleaded his age and bodily infirmities. So he was married in spite of himself to his nun, and showed his disposition to make the best of it by making her a wedding-present of his new Latin treatise, just finished, on *The Origin of Evil*, and receiving in tender return a Greek copy of the *Philippics* of Demosthenes. Three years later the wretched woman was accused of adultery, and being put to the torture confessed her crime and was drowned in a sack, while her paramour was beheaded. Bonivard, being questioned, declared his belief of her innocence, and that her worst faults were that she wanted to make him too pious, and tormented him to begin preaching, and sometimes beat him when he had a few friends in to drink.*

For five years after this catastrophe the old man lingered, tended by hirelings, but watched with filial gratitude by the little state whose liberties he had helped to save, and whose heroic history he has recorded.

---

* This touching tribute of conjugal affection is all the more honorable to Bonivard from the fact that this wife, like the others, had provoked him. Only a few months before he had been compelled to appear before the consistory to answer for treating her in a public place with profane and abusive language, applying to her some French term which is expressed in the record only by abbreviations.

He had at least the comfort of having finished that great work; and when he brought the manuscript of it to the council, they referred it to a committee with Master Calvin at the head; who reported that it was written in a rude and familiar style, quite beneath the dignity of history, and that for this and other reasons it had better not be printed. The precious manuscript was laid on the shelf until in the lapse of years it was found that the very reasons why those solemn critics rejected it were the things that gave it supreme value to a later age. It has been the pride of Geneva scholars to print in elegant archaic style every page written by the Prisoner of Chillon in prose or verse, on history, polity, philology and theology.*

---

* Like every subject relating to the history of Geneva, the life of Bonivard has been thoroughly studied by local antiquarians and historians. The most important work on the subject is that of Dr. Chaponnière, before cited; this is reprinted (but without the documents attached) as a preface to the new edition of the *Chronicles*. M. Edmond Chevrier, in a slight pamphlet (Macon, 1868), gives a critical account both of the man and of his writings. Besides these may be named Vulliemin: *Chillon Etude historique*, Lausanne, 1851; J. Gaberel: *Le Château de Chillon et Bonivard*. Geneva. Marc Monnier, *Genève et ses Poètes* (Geneva, 1847), gives an excellent criticism on Bonivard as author. For original materials consult besides the work of Chaponnière) Galiffe: *Matériaux pour l'Histoire de Genève*, and Cramer; *Notes extraites des Registres du Consistoire*, a rare book in lithography (Geneva, 1853). A weak little article in the *Catholic World* for September, 1876, bravely attacks Bonivard as "one of the Protestant models of virtue," and triumphantly proves him to have been far from perfect. The charge, however, that he was "a traitor to his ecclesiastical character," and "quitted

Somewhere about September, 1570, Francis Bonivard died, aged seventy-seven, lonely and childless, leaving the city his heir. The cherished collection of books that was the comfort of his harassed life has grown into the library of a university, and the little walled town for whose ancient liberties he ventured such perils and suffered such imprisonment is, and for the three hundred years since has been, one of the chief radiant centres of light and liberty for all the world.

---

his convent and broke his vows," is founded on a blunder. Bonivard never took monastic vows or holy orders, but held his living *in commendam*, as a layman. The main resource, however, for Bonivard's life up to his liberation from Chillon is in his own works, especially the *Chronicles* (Geneva, edition Fick, 1867).

WM. LLOYD GARRISON

WILLIAM LLOYD GARRISON.

Having frequent occasion, in the prosecution of certain historical studies, to refer to the voluminous biography of Mr. Garrison, written by two of his sons,* we find the question again and again recurring: What idea of the man and his times would be got from these volumes by one who had no other source of information?

It is a question not altogether easy to answer off-hand. Doubtless the idea would be somewhat confused at first; but being allowed to settle and clarify itself, after some cancelling of contradictions and eliminating of impossibilities, it would come out somewhat in this shape:

Mr. Garrison was a man of meek, gentle and affectionate spirit, and wholly blameless character, who devoted himself at an early age, with absolute unselfishness, to universal philanthropy, and especially to the abolition of slavery. Beginning this work with a nearly unanimous public sentiment on his side, he pushed it forward

* "William Lloyd Garrison: 1805-1879. The Story of his Life told by his Children." New York: The Century Co. 1885, 1889.

with such boldness, ability, tact and discretion, that by the end of fifteen years he had brought the public opinion of the nation, both South and North, into almost equally unanimous antagonism to himself. Particularly was this true of the Christian Church and ministry in America, who had shown him hearty sympathy at first; but many of whom, including men who are even yet held in the highest veneration and love, actually engaged in active opposition to slavery with the nefarious purpose of thereby sustaining that wicked institution; and when Mr. Garrison, in the simple fulfilment of his duty, rebuked such conduct, they abused him, the gentle Garrison, with vituperative language. This conspiracy of the entire Christian Church against him, simply for his superior righteousness, was only exceeded in wickedness by the abominable conduct of many of his nearest friends and benefactors and most self-sacrificing fellow-laborers, who had the hardihood to separate from his Society, and set up another society and newspaper which they called anti-slavery, but which the acumen of Mr. Garrison at once recognized as "the worst form of pro-slavery." Thus, deserted and betrayed by men whom for years he had extolled as among the noblest of the human race, he was publicly declared at last, by one of his few remaining adherents, to be "the only righteous in a world perverse."

In nothing was this good man's abhorrence of slavery more shiningly illustrated than in his rejection of any slavish bondage to his own consistency. At some periods in his career he was a gradual abolitionist, a gradual emancipationist, a colonizationist, in favor of compensated emancipation, devoted to the Constitution of the United States, inculcating the exercise of citizenship, and maintaining a narrow and rigid Sabbatarianism. He had held these views in the simplicity and innocence of his heart; but such was the wild and swift degeneracy of the age and people, that after he laid them down, they were never afterwards held by anybody else, except with vile insincerity, by patent fallacy, with abominable motives, for atrocious ends.

His methods as a reformer were original almost to the point of paradox. He had two main objects: 1, Immediate emancipation of slaves by their holders; 2, immediate abolition of slavery by the repeal of the slave code. The first was sought by a style of address to the slaveholders that enraged every man of them against him and his views to the utmost fury. The second was to be achieved by persuading all opponents of slavery into abdicating their rights and powers as citizens, and so committing the control of legislation exclusively to the upholders of that iniquitous system. But in the prosecution of this bold and energetic policy, the good Garrison was sadly hindered by the criminal folly of those who thought that one good way to oppose bad laws in a republic was to vote against them, and who thus committed themselves to "the worst and most dangerous form of pro-slavery."

But nothing in all this good man's career was so wonderful as his success. At last, by the power of his "sweet reasonableness," he so far won the people of the free States to sympathy with his abhorrence of the Constitution and Union of the United States and his sense of the sinfulness of voting, that they formed a great political party in which every principle characteristic of Mr. Garrison was repudiated, and fought out at the polls the old issue, that was old when Garrison was a baby. But his greatest triumph was when his peace and non-resistance principles had gained such a hold over the popular mind, that at last a million of men stood in arms and entered into the bloodiest war of recent times for the maintenance of the Union and Constitution which Mr. Garrison detested —a war in which every death was held by him to be a wicked murder, and the incidental result of which was the abolition of slavery.

It was a fitting close to this triumphant career, that when he had accomplished his great work, he for himself and his family and friends in his behalf, should step promptly forward as they have, to accept for him the homage due to successful and humane achievement.

Such is the paradoxical, but filially pious portraiture of Mr. Garrison given in these volumes. The hero of them is depicted as a noble and wholly faultless character, of whom the world was not worthy. Indeed it is hardly so much the worthiness of the hero as the world's unworthiness of him that most impresses the reader's mind. One who reads believing is shocked, from page to page, with growing proofs of the utter debasement and turpitude of the generation in which he lived, especially of those who pass for the best men of it; and with the vile perfidy towards Mr. Garrison of such large numbers of those who came into intimate relations with him, in business, in reform-agitation, and in personal friendship.

No trait of Mr. Garrison's character is more emphasized and illustrated by his biographers than his singular equanimity, self-control and gentleness of temper. His mildness of manner and expression are the theme of repeated and admiring comment; and it is demonstrated, not boastfully perhaps, but with evident pride, that his remarkable composure, in circumstances which to most men would have been exciting to the last degree, was due not to self-control, but to the actual absence of excitement. Contrariwise to the public impression of him, he was not a man of hasty or irritable temper, or given to grudges or evil thoughts of others, but one who cherished not merely a doctrine of non-resistance, but actual kindly feelings towards bitter enemies. And yet, as we read, we do come upon language of his that has a different sound. For instance, in a long article on the remonstrances of some of his best friends and fellow-reformers against what they deemed the harshness and severity of his language, he says :

"The same cuckoo cry is raised against me now as I heard when I stood forth alone; and the same sagacious predictions and grave admonitions are uttered now as were then spoken with the infallibility of ignorance, the disinterestedness of cowardice, and the prudence of imbecility. There are many calling themselves anti-slavery men who, because they are only 'half-fledged' themselves, and have neither the strength nor the courage to soar, must needs flutter and scream because my spirit will not stoop in its flight heavenward, and come down to their filthy nest."—[Vol. I. 459, 460.]

Improving upon this pleasing metaphor, he characterizes the General Conference of the Methodist Church as "a cage of unclean birds, and synagogue of Satan." [II. 78.] The action of the Consociation of Rhode Island in declining to entertain a memorial from an epicene convention in Boston is declared to be "clerical ruffianism." [II. 220, n.] And the Rev. Charles T. Torrey, who not long after died a martyr to his anti-slavery convictions in the Baltimore jail, but who had been guilty of the "sedition" (so Mr. Garrison termed it) of desiring another Society and another journal than Garrison's is described as coming in "the full tide of his priestly bile." [II. 270.] We have these occasional specimens of a style of expression which in most men would be indicative of anger, or hatred, or some evil passion, although in

this book no evidence appears, except in
expressions of shame, disgust and heart-
sickness on the part of many of Garrison's
best friends, that his habitual style was
that of the most brutally vituperative writer
of his time. And yet the testimony, both
of himself and of others who knew him, is
that he was a man of exceptional mildness
and gentleness of temper. What solution
can be found for so strange a paradox?

That which is suggested by one of his
admiring friends and cited by his biographers, seems not improbable. Miss Harriet
Martineau, in 1835, found his countenance
to be

"wholly expressive of purity, animation and
gentleness." "His conversation . . . is of
the most practical cast. . . . Sagacity is the
most striking attribute of his conversation. It
has none of the severity, the harshness, the bad
taste of his writing; it is as gladsome as his
countenance, and as gentle as his voice. Through
the whole of his deportment breathes the evidence of a heart at ease. . . . I do not pre-
tend to like or to approve the tone of Garrison's
printed censures. I could not use such language
myself towards any class of offenders, nor can
I sympathize in its use by others. But it is only
fair to mention that Garrison *adopts it warily;*
and that I am persuaded that he is elevated
above passion and has no unrighteous anger to
vent in harsh expressions. . . . He gives his
reasons for his severity with a calmness, meek-

ness and softness which contrast strongly with the subject of the discourse, and which convince the objector that there is *principle* at the bottom of the practice."—[II. 70–71.]

It seems a hard thing for sons to have to say of a father whom they love and venerate, and yet it seems to be true, that the frenzied and unbridled scurrility of Garrison's polemic, such as might be extenuated, not excused, on the ground of irritated feeling or excited passion, was really adopted by him "warily," without a particle of animosity, in cold blood, as a matter of policy for the accomplishment of a purpose. There was no noble and irrepressible rage in it. His feelings never ran away with him, no matter how diabolical the wickedness that confronted him. A very striking illustration of this self-command is presented in these volumes. On the subject of liquor-selling, said he, in 1829:

"We who are somewhat impetuous in our disposition and singular in our notions of reform— who are so uncharitable as to make no distinction between men engaged in one common traffic, which shall excuse the destroyer of thousands and heap contumely on the murderer of a dozen—we demand that the whole truth be told on all occasions, whether it induces persecution or occasions a breach of private friendship. . . . If it be injurious, or criminal, or dangerous, or disreputable to drink ardent spirits, it is far more so to vend, or distil, or import this liquid fire. 'Woe unto him who putteth the cup to his neighbor's lips'—who increases his wealth at the expense of the bodies and souls of men —who takes away the bread of the poor and devours the earnings of industry—who scatters his poison through the veins and arteries of the community, till even the grave is burdened with his victims! Against *him* must the artillery of public indignation be brought to bear; and the decree must go forth, as from the lips of Jehovah, that he who will deal in the accursed article can lay no claim to honesty of purpose or holiness of life, but is a shameless enemy to the happiness and prosperity of his fellow-creatures."—[I. 155, 156.]

"He looked upon 'every distiller or vender of ardent spirits' as 'a poisoner of the health and morals of community'; and could even say, in his address in 1832 before the second annual Convention of the People of Color in Philadelphia: 'God is my witness that great as is my detestation of slavery and the foreign slave trade, I had rather be a slaveholder—yea, a kidnapper on the African coast—than sell this poison to my fellow-creatures for common consumption.'"—[I. 268.]

This was in 1832. In 1833, this uncompromising reformer, burning with holy indignation, had the golden opportunity of confronting, in the midst of his ill-gotten and blood-stained wealth, one of the most notorious of these monsters, more detestable than the slaveholder and the kidnapper, these murderers and public poisoners, of whom he was resolved to speak the truth on all occasions however embarrassing. It was a peculiarly flagrant case, for the caitiff wretch had not only openly made and sold his liquid damnation, but had commended it to his neighbors' lips in that seductive form known as Buxton's Entire; and nevertheless, was holding a high position in the public esteem, and giving himself the airs of a philanthropist and reformer and Christian. In all Mr. Garrison's stormy career, he never had so good an opportunity for unlimbering the "artillery of indignation" for a point-blank shot. But instead of this he speaks with undisguised delight of a "polite invitation by letter" from this ogre "to take breakfast with him"; on which occasion our reformer, instead of warning his host of the hypocrisy of his "claim of honesty of purpose or holiness of life" and faithfully denouncing him as the "shameless enemy of his fellow-creatures," accepted his breakfast and his compliments without a syllable of protest; and after returning to America, described him as "the worthy successor of Wilberforce, our esteemed friend and coadjutor, Thomas Fowell Buxton," and declares that, aside from a single mistake of anti-slavery policy, "Mr. Buxton deserves universal admiration and gratitude for his long-continued, able and disinterested efforts, amidst severe ridicule and malignant opposition, to break every yoke and set the oppressed free."—[I. 351, 352.]

Miss Martineau was right. The spirit of the prophet was completely subject unto the prophet. He was able to restrain the fury of his indignation against this monstrous criminal, and devote all his energies, in England, to hounding, pestering and abusing the agent of a benevolent enterprise, of which less than four years before, Garrison himself had been an extravagant eulogist. The Colonization agent was guilty of not keeping up with Garrison in the nimble changes of his mind from love to hate; and this was a crime as much worse than Buxton's as Buxton's was worse than that of the slaveholder and the kidnapper. But let it not be supposed that even this badgering of the Colonization agent was a matter of indignation. As Miss Martineau perceived, it was only "sagacity"—part of a course "adopted warily," and on "principle"—a course disgusting enough to her, as well as to Whittier, and Follen, and the Tappans, and many others, but which nevertheless, as he calmly explained, with "gladsome countenance" and "gentle voice," had to be pursued as a matter of policy.

It is not impossible to comprehend the situation in which Mr. Garrison felt himself drawn or driven to this disgraceful policy. We must remember how scanty were the resources not only material and social, but intellectual, with which he entered on his crusade. He was a decidedly bright young fellow, who had worked his way up from printer's boy to editor—wrote in a fairly good English style, with a knack for turning a sonnet which now and then rose to the dignity of real poetry. But he lacked intellectual strength, and was conscious of the lack. The reader of this book is impressed, in the pages from Garrison's pen, with the absence of genuine eloquence, or vigor of argument, or acuteness of observation. A superiority of intellectual and moral tone is recognized at once, when we pass from a page of Garrison's writing to a page from Elizur Wright, or even Lewis Tappan. Now, what do most men do in this case—conscious that their strength is inadequate to their undertaking? They are commonly tempted to make up in violence for the defect of strength. And this was the temptation to which Garrison yielded. He was always straining his voice till it broke into falsetto. He might not be able to argue successfully; but he could scold like a fishwife. He might not convict his adversary of wrong; but he could pelt him with hard names. He might not be able to command the attention of the people by weight of character or power of language; but he could infuriate them by insult. Here were cheap substitutes for eloquence always at hand, and he had small scruple about using them. He might not be able to win any large following to serve under him by the attraction of his genius, or the success of his leadership; but perhaps some might be intimidated into his service by a policy of systematic insult. So this policy was deliberately adopted and persistently followed. Probably it was the first instance of an attempt to carry forward a scheme of Christian philanthropy in main reliance on blackmail. The bitterest epithets and most damaging accusations in Mr. Garrison's extensive repertory were applied to those who were nearest him but failed to adhere to him. The one lower grade of turpitude was that of the men who, having once trained in his troop, detached themselves from it. The "worst and most dangerous form of pro-slavery" was to be an anti-slavery man outside of Garrison's residuary faction. There was no lack of collaborators to whom the policy of Garrison was congenial, and it was industriously prosecuted. Faithful citizens, and especially Christian ministers, were studiously annoyed with false charges of being "pro-slavery." Americans going abroad found that a system of correspondence was in operation by which evil reports were sent in advance of them. But the delight of the Garrison press and platform was to seize the occasion of the recent death of some exceptionally beloved and honored citizen, when hearts were tender, and the wounds of bereavement not yet closed, to defile his fresh grave with some abominable accusation. And down almost to this very day it has been the amiable practice of some of the survivors of that faction, notably of Mr. Oliver Johnson, to signalize the departure of some man honored for his great services in the cause of human freedom, by printing mendacious charges against him of pro-slavery sympathy, and sending them marked to the mourners.

It is only by glimpses between the lines that the reader of this biography gets an idea of the state of public sentiment in

America at the time when Garrison began his work. Garrison's own reckless and swaggering account of it is this:

"At that time [before the beginning of *The Liberator* in 1831] there was scarcely a man in all the land who dared to peep or mutter on the subject of slavery; the pulpit and the press were dumb; no anti-slavery organizations were made; no public addresses were delivered; no reproofs, no warnings, no entreaties were uttered in the ears of the people, silence, almost unbroken silence, prevailed universally."—[I. 458.]

In the same ridiculously false and braggart tone is his talk about Channing's little work on slavery: "We do claim all that is sound or valuable in the book as *our own;* its sole excellences are its *moral plagiarisms;*"—[II. 89]. Habitually, he abounds with great swelling words of assumption that he is the very founder and inventor of anti-slavery feeling, argument and effort.

And yet throughout the book, and especially the earlier part of it, we come continually upon facts that are only to be explained by supposing (what is the demonstrable truth) that Garrison from his childhood grew up in an atmosphere of abhorrence of slavery—an atmosphere which pervaded the North and, to a large extent the South as well. The really remarkable and distinguishing thing about his early life is the torpid insensibility of his own conscience on this subject, while all about him men were feeling deeply and speaking and acting boldly. He had had exceptional opportunities of knowing slavery in its most hideous aspect, in successive visits to one of the chief slave markets of the country; but he took no interest in the matter. In the year 1826, a speech was made in Congress by Mr. Everett, which seemed to apologize for slavery; Mr. Gurley, of the Colonization Society, Mr. Bacon, and other friends of the colored people broke out in indignant protest and denunciation; Mr. Garrison copied the speech into his newspaper without the slightest sign of disapproval.

When, at last, his sluggish conscience was roused to recognize that slavery was wrong, and he began to speak and act, he found that the whole country was beforehand with him. In the year 1828, he refers, in his Bennington newspaper, to a petition recently presented to Congress by more than a thousand residents of the District of Columbia, including all the District Judges, praying for the abolition of slavery in the District. And presently a meeting is convened at the Bennington Academy at which a petition for the same object, drawn by Garrison's hand, is read and adopted, which reads:

"Your petitioners deem it unnecessary to attempt to maintain by elaborate arguments that the existence of slavery is highly detrimental to the happiness, peace and prosperity of that nation in whose bosom and under whose auspices it is nourished; and especially that it is inconsistent with the spirit of our government and laws. All this is readily admitted *by every patriot and Christian*. . . . It is gratifying to believe that *a large majority of the inhabitants of the District, and also of our more Southern brethren, are earnest for the abolition*. . . . Your petitioners deem it preposterous that while there is one half of the States in which slavery does not exist, and while *a large majority of our white population are desirous of seeing it extirpated*, this evil is suffered to canker in the vitals of the republic."

The petition was sent to *all the postmasters* of the State of Vermont, with the request that they would obtain signatures to it; and most of them "responded nobly"; so that the document was sent to Washington with no less than 2352 signatures, and there found a *nearly unanimous* resolution of the Pennsylvania House of Representatives in favor of the same object.— [I. 109, 110.]

It is this exact period of which it is impudently declared (for the greater glory of Garrison):

"Fifty years ago [*i. e.*, in 1829], it is no exaggeration to say, this nation, in church and state, from President to boot-black—I mean the white boot-black—was thoroughly pro-slavery. In the Sodom there might have been a Lot or two here and there—some profound thinker who wished justice to be done though the heavens should fall, but he was despondent. It seemed as though nearly the whole business of the press, the pulpit and the theological seminary was to reconcile the people to the permanent degradation and slavery of the negro race."—[I. 298. Quoted from a speech of Elizur Wright, in June, 1879.]

Who would suppose, from reading this statement of history, that Garrison's boyhood had passed in the midst of an anti-slavery agitation that convulsed the nation almost to the point of civil war; or that in 1818 that noble act of the Presbyterian Church declaring slavery to be "a gross violation of the most precious and sacred rights of human nature, utterly inconsistent with the law of God, and totally irreconcilable with the spirit and principles of the gospel of Christ," had been *unanimously* adopted by the General Assembly, representing North and South? The eulogists of Garrison will hardly have the effrontery to claim that it was from their hero that the illustrious Kentuckian, Robert J. Breckenridge, learned either the ethics or the rhetoric of that splendid invective which he uttered in 1833 in the pages of the "Biblical Repertory," in which he declared "slavery as it is daily exhibited in every slave State" to be "a system which is utterly indefensible on every correct human principle, and utterly abhorrent from every law of God"; in which rebuking the apologists of the institution he exclaims: "Out upon such folly! The man who cannot see that involuntary domestic slavery, as it exists among us, is founded on the principle of taking by force that which is another's, has simply no moral sense"; . . . "these are reasons for a Christian land to look upon and then ask: Can any system which they are advanced to defend be compatible with virtue and truth? . . . Hereditary slavery is without pretence, except in avowed rapacity."

Such views as these, of a conspicuous leader of public opinion in the slave States in 1833, instead of being, according to the preposterous assumption of Mr. Garrison's admirers, something unknown before his advent, devised by his own heart, becoming prevalent through his propagation of them, were, as a matter of exact history, the generally prevalent sentiment of the country at the beginning of his career; and the progressive decline of them, and, at the South, the practical extinction of them, synchronizes with the progress of Mr. Garrison's anti-slavery operations. Whether these operations stood to the decline of anti-slavery sentiment in the relation of cause to effect is a fair question, on which, however, in our own minds, there is not a particle of doubt. It is clear to us that Mr. Garrison and his propaganda had no small part in the demoralization of public opinion which went on to worse and worse during the period of his greatest activity.

But while he had no originality in the advocacy of anti-slavery, of emancipation, or of abolition—on all these points merely accepting the general sentiment of good men prevalent at the beginning of his career—there were two favorite nostrums on which he claimed exclusive rights, at least for the American market; one of these he labelled "immediate emancipation," and the other "immediate abolition." Both of them were founded in fallacy—that form of fallacy which one of his surviving disciples, Mr. Oliver Johnson, with unconscious humor, characterized * as "elastic definition," but which is better known to logicians as "ambiguous middle." All slaveholding is wicked, said the reformer; therefore every slaveholder should instantly emancipate all his slaves, and until he does so, he is a murderer, a man-stealer, a pirate, to be excommunicated from the Church, and shunned by decent men. But being questioned what he would do in the case of one who was holding slaves only until he could bring them away to a State where the laws would permit the emancipation of them, he answers at once: "When I say slaveholding is wicked, I mean the wicked kind of slaveholding; the man you describe holds slaves, indeed, but he is not what I mean by a slaveholder. I have 'an elastic definition' that can be accommodated to all such cases." In short, he fell afoul of the English language; his long quarrel with the best men of his generation was a contest in defence of his indefeasible right to use words out of their proper meaning.

. So with his demand for "immediate abolition," objection to which filled him with "inexpressible abhorrence and dismay." It "does not mean," he says, "that the

---
* *Century Magazine,* vol. IV. (1883) pp. 153, 636.

slaves shall immediately . . . be free from the benevolent restraints of guardianship."—[I. 294.] In short, when he says "immediate abolition" he means what is ordinarily understood by "gradual abolition," which if any man dare to express approval of, he will belabor him with foul words in his *Liberator* and do what he can to injure him in public estimation.

With more patience than this patent fallacy deserved, the sober anti-slavery men of this country labored to clear excited minds of the illusion which Garrison and his followers persistently labored to maintain. Said Leonard Bacon:

"As for the thing which alone they profess to recognize as slavery, we hold it to be invariably sinful. As for the thing which, when they attempt to speak accurately, they call emancipation, we hold it to be the plainest and first duty of every master. As for the thing which they describe as the meaning of immediate abolition, we hold it to be not only practicable and safe, but the very first thing to be done for the safety of a slaveholding country. The immediate abolition against which we protest as perilous to the commonwealth and unjust to the slaves, is a different thing from that which the immediate abolitionists think they are urging on the country. . . .

"The sophism by which they unwittingly impose on their own minds and inflame the minds of others, is this: the terms 'slavery,' 'slaveholding,' 'immediate emancipation,' etc. have one meaning in their definitions, and, to a great and unavoidable extent, another meaning in their denunciations and popular harangues. Thus they define a slaveholder to be one who claims and treats his fellow-men as property—as things—as destitute of all personal rights; one, in a word, whose criminality is self-evident. But the moment they begin to speak of slaveholders in the way of declamation, the word which they have strained out of its proper import springs back to its position, and denotes any man who stands in the relation of overseer and governor to those whom the law has constituted slaves; and consequently every man who, in the meaning of the laws, or in the meaning of common parlance, is a slaveholder, is denounced with unmeasured expressions of abhorrence and hate, as an enemy of the species. What is the effect of this on their own minds? What, on the minds of those who happen, from one cause or another, to be ripe for factious or fanatical excitement against the South? What, on the minds of those who, without unravelling the sophistry of the case, know that many a slaveholder is conscientious, and does regard his slaves as brethren? What, on the minds of those slaveholders themselves who are conscious of no such criminality"—*Quarterly Christian Spectator*, 1834.

The possible effect of his sophistical talk on other men's minds seems not to have been veiled from Mr. Garrison. In the retrospect, at least, he looked back with complacency to the syllogism which he had furnished to the extreme defenders of slavery : "If human beings could be justly held in bondage for one hour, they could be for days and weeks and years, and so on indefinitely from generation to generation."—[I. 140.] It was an instruction which needed no bettering, to fit it exactly to the use of pro-slavery men, North or South, in their conflict with the anti-slavery feeling that was everywhere dominant when Garrison began his glorious work. But this bearing of it seemed to be no objection to it in Mr. Garrison's mind; and the fact that it would be exasperating and alienating to good, conscientious and antislavery men among the slaveholders was vastly in its favor. His grievance with the old anti-slavery societies was that they did not "personally arraign the slaveholder and hold him criminal for not immediately emancipating his slaves, and seek to make him odious and put him beyond the pale of intercourse."—[I. 159, *note*. The language is the biographers'.]

Nothing in all this book is more truly characteristic of Mr. Garrison than these words of his children. A policy of reform might be wise, effective, successful; it might have extinguished slavery, as indeed it had extinguished it, in State after State, and be moving hopefully for the like result in other States yet; but unless it was personally exasperating it had no charms for him. He was not exasperated himself; and he no more believed every slaveholder to be criminal than Dr. Bacon or Dr. Breckenridge did; but with his little contrivance of "an elastic definition" he continued, with great composure and equanimity, to pour out the weekly torrent of bitter, foul, insulting language with which he succeeded in quenching the anti-slavery sentiment of the South to its last embers, and infuriating an opposition to the very name of abolitionist, even in the North, that showed itself in the shameful mobs which he delighted to provoke, and which were repressed or prevented by the efforts of men for whom he had no thanks, but only abuse and calumny. His love of a mob was not in the least like the Tipperary Irishman's delight in a shillalah-fight. It was a matter of policy, and in the roughest tumble of it his "mind was tranquil"; and when it was over he sat down and footed up the net advantages: "New subscribers to the *Liberator* continue to come in—not less than a dozen to-day. Am much obliged to the mob."—[II. 50.] He was even capable of refraining from exciting a mob when he saw no profit in it—"a mob without doing us any benefit, as the market is now getting to be somewhat glutted with deeds of violence." —[II. 105.] But in general, he actually hungered for a row, and labored, when he saw the populace nearing the boiling-point, to throw in fresh provocations, and invite general attention to his non-resistance principles. On the eve of the Boston riot, he was disgusted with the apparent lull of popular excitement which threatened that the storm would blow over. "Boston is beginning to sink into apathy. The reaction has come rapidly, but we are trying to get the steam up again."—[II. 2.] In like manner, at the dedication of Pennsylvania Hall in Philadelphia, his disgust at the address of David Paul Brown, the eminent anti-slavery lawyer, was irrepressible. That address seemed adapted "to allay, in some measure, the prejudice that prevails against us and our holy cause"; and that was not at all what he had come to Philadelphia for. There were placards out inciting to a riot, and it was an opportunity not to be missed. The mob needed punching up, and Garrison was just the man to do it. So he took the platform with some sneering and insulting remarks about Mr. Brown and his address, and about men of "caution," and "prudence," and "judiciousness," generally.

"Sir, I have learned to hate those words. . . . Sir, slavery will not be overthrown without excitement, a most tremendous excitement. And let me say there is too much quietude in this city. It shows that the upholders of this wicked system have not yet felt that their favorite sin has been much endangered. You need and must have a moral earthquake. . . . Your cause will not prosper here—the philosophy of reform forbids you to expect it—until it excites popular tumult, and brings down upon it a shower of brickbats and rotten eggs, and it is threatened with a coat of tar-and-feathers."— [II. 215, 216, *note*.]

The desire of Garrison's heart was promptly gratified by the smashing of the windows and the burning of the building; out of all which he got safely off, and wrote to his mother-in-law in high spirits, from Boston. " We have had great doings in Philadelphia, during the present week. . . . It will do incalculable good to our cause. . . . Our friends are all in excellent spirits, shouting Alleluia! for the Lord God omnipotent reigneth! Let the earth rejoice!"

The attitude of Mr. Garrison and his

queer little "persecuted remnant" of followers, towards the mob, was like that of Messrs. Dodson and Fogg towards the enraged Mr. Pickwick. "'Perhaps you would like to call us swindlers, sir,' said Dodson. 'Pray do, sir, if you feel disposed; now pray do, sir.' 'Go on, sir; do go on,' added Mr. Fogg. 'You had better call us thieves, sir; or perhaps you would like to assault one of us. Pray do it, if you would; we will not make the smallest resistance. Pray do it, sir'; and Fogg put himself very temptingly within the reach of Mr. Pickwick's clenched fist."

The case is not exactly in point. The mob was by no means as innocent as Mr. Pickwick, and the abusive epithets, to which *thief* and *swindler* were terms of compliment, were rather bestowed by Mr. Garrison than solicited. But Dodson and Fogg never equalled Mr. Garrison in the cool studiousness with which he invited assault with the standing promise of impunity, serenely calculating on the ulterior advantage of it. He swaggered insolently about in the panoply of his non-resistance principles, the "Moral Bully" described by Dr. Holmes:

" His velvet throat against thy corded wrist,
  His loosened tongue against thy doubled fist."

" The *Moral Bully*, though he never swears,
Nor kicks intruders down his entry stairs,
Though meekness plants his backward-sloping
   hat,
And non-resistance ties his white cravat, . . .
Hugs the same passion to his narrow breast;
That heaves the cuirass on the trooper's
   chest;
Feels the same comfort, while his acrid words
Turn the sweet milk of kindness into curds,
As the scarred ruffian of the pirate's deck
When his long swivel rakes the staggering
   wreck."

The lesson of Mr. Garrison's life, truly told, is instructive but sad. It is the story of the failure and wreck of what could hardly, in any case, have been a great career, but might have been a wholly honorable and useful one. The whole course of his active life is a continuous history of opportunities wasted, influence forfeited, faithful friends and benefactors alienated and forced into hostility, and friends that still remained "sickened" at the folly and violence of his language, and at the irreparable mischiefs wrought by it to the cause which he claimed for his own. Meanwhile he was embittered by seeing "enlargement and deliverance arise from another place." The sober, conscientious, Christian anti-slavery sentiment of the country was clearly enlightened, and resolutely and wisely led, by such men as Albert Barnes, Leonard Bacon, William Ellery Channing and Francis Wayland— men for whose persons, whose arguments, and whose measures Mr. Garrison had no words but bitter denunciation and insult, and all the more as he saw them leading on to success where he had miserably failed. The attempt to represent that the only consistent and sincere anti-slavery of the nation was confined to Garrison and the infinitesimal faction of his adherents —an attempt pertinaciously prosecuted by him during his lifetime, and now renewed since his death—needs to be rebuked in the name of public morality; and not less, the mischievous lesson that is deduced from this false representation, to wit, that extravagant statement, sweeping denunciation and personal abuse of antagonists may be relied on to carry almost any crotchet of "reform," if only they are stuck to long enough.

The public career of Mr. Garrison, to which we have mainly confined our attention, is not difficult to understand. His personal character as exhibited in this book would be a more complicated study, very interesting, but less important to the world. Certain fine qualities he had in a high degree. His courage lacked nothing, but a little modesty, of being perfect and entire; but he advertised it too much in his newspaper. He was completely superior to mercenary considerations, and took joyfully the spoiling of his own goods, and still more joyfully the spoiling of other people's goods ; no one of the proprietors of Pennsylvania Hall seems to havee qualled him in the happy serenity and even hilarity with which he witnessed the destruction of that valuable property. For the great cause which he had at heart, he was willing to bear the loss of friends—so willing, in fact, that as they turned, grieved or indignant, from his door, he usually kicked them down the steps, only not with an actual boot of leather—that he held to be sinful. His sympathy with the slaves was deep and sincere; the groans of their prolonged bondage were torture to his soul; yet even this torture he was willing to bear cheerfully for an indefinite period (no matter what their preference might be) rather than have them emancipated on incorrect principles [I. 348, 352]; so far was he from being a reckless enthusiast in his humanity. Conscious of superiority to such vulgar forms of selfishness, he sincerely thought himself (there is much evidence of this, sometimes pathetic, sometimes amusing) to be a perfect man.

One is surprised and almost sorry to find it claimed for him that he was not passionate or vindictive—that when he was running amuck through society, striking and stabbing indiscriminately all but those that ran with him, it was a mere matter of policy, about which he chatted "gladsomely" with his friends. In like manner, we are pained to discover that he was far from being the pachyderm which his recklessness of the feelings and reputations of others indicates him to be. He is sensitive to the pains which he delights to inflict or see inflicted on other men. If he fairly chuckles with joy at preventing the Colonizationists from getting a place for their meeting [I. 450] it is not because he does not go bemoaning the wickedness of the churches in not being willing to lend him or his friends a meetinghouse gratis. His devoted labors to make other people "odious, and put them beyond the pale of intercourse," were compatible with bitter complaints that he found he had made himself odious instead. The most abusive of writers is continually grumbling at being abused. He calls on John Breckenridge, who loses his temper and becomes "really abusive"; Garrison bears it with a grieved and injured spirit, but with angelic meekness, goes home and down on his knees for his enemy; and then puts the knife into him in the next *Liberator* as "ferocious and diabolical."—[I. 449.]

Mr. Garrison's religious faith, through the earlier period of his life, seems genuine, deep and practical. Not Archbishop Laud, nor Saint Peter Arbuez, gives evidence of a more honest piety, or more strikingly illustrates Isaac Taylor's definition of fanaticism, as the combination of the religious sentiment with the malignant passions.

For the materials of this exposition of the character and career of Mr. Garrison, it has not been necessary to go outside of the voluminous biography written of him by his own sons. No one can blame them for not having told the whole story. They have told enough to make their huge book refute itself. Can it be wondered at that they should have walked backward laying a garment upon both their shoulders, so as not to see their father's shame? But sooner or later some severely just and faithful hand must take up the task of thoroughly exposing the perversions of history that have been perpetrated by a considerable number of writers, for the canonization of Garrison. It is in the interest of good morals that he should be known to the next generation, as he was known to the past generation, as the systematic, cold-blooded and unscrupulous calumniator of better men than himself, and the constant antagonist of the men and the measures that were most helpful (as the event demonstrated) to the abolition of slavery. That his example may not be of evil influence in the future, it is needful that the demonstrable fact should be publicly exhibited and proved, that good did not come from the evil which he did that good might come; that the cause which he claimed as his own was begun without him, and went forward to success not because of him but in spite of him; and that the failure of his career— a miserable failure, notwithstanding all the false glorying of his panegyrists—is a warning to any who may hereafter be tempted of the devil to follow him in those methods which won for him the indelible title of "malignant philanthropist." This work might well occupy a volume, or more than one. But something may be accomplished towards it, even within the narrow limits of a magazine article.

II.

The common account of Mr. Garrison's career is to this effect: That he found the country, and especially the Christian Church and ministry, sunken in a deep and criminal apathy concerning the condition of the negro population of America, both slave and free; that by his earnest and powerful appeals he succeeded in arousing the public conscience to the sinfulness of slavery, and enlisting its sympathies with his cause; that the principles which he enunciated, the measures which he advocated, and the men whom he drew around him and organized for action, became effective at last of the abolition of slavery.

The demonstrable facts of history are these: At the time of the strangely tardy awakening of Mr. Garrison's conscience to the wrongfulness of slavery, there was a generally prevalent and growing anti-slavery sentiment both at the North and at the South, and this sentiment was especially active in the Christian Church and ministry;

it continued active on the same principles
and along similar lines of effort with those
under which freedom had already been secured
to one-half of the Union, and was
operating hopefully in several of the border
slave States; it was effecting emancipations
from year to year by the hundred and the
thousand; it was zealous in promoting the
welfare of the free blacks. The new principles,
measures and methods inaugurated by
Mr. Garrison had no effect on the general
anti-slavery sentiment of the country except
to defeat its enterprises at the North, and to
extinguish it at the South; they procured
the abolition or mitigation of slavery in no
single State, and, so far as known, the
emancipation of no single slave; the peaceful,
constitutional and legal measures for resisting
the spread of slavery that were undertaken
in the interest of freedom were in
succession steadfastly resisted by Mr. Garrison
and his men; the notable and successful
leaders in the anti-slavery conflict were by
him, with few exceptions, discredited and
vilified; when, in spite of him, the advance
of slavery had been barred by the colonizing
of Kansas, no resource was left to the friends
of slavery but secession and war; when secession
came, Mr. Garrison took sides with the
secessionists; when war was begun, he was

in favor of surrender. If Mr. Garrison could have won the anti-slavery people of the North into sympathy with his notions, slavery would have been dominant to-day throughout the entire country. Unhappily, in alienating the people of the country from himself and from his odious peculiarities, he alienated them also from the cause which he misrepresented; and succeeded in nothing so much as in making the very name of abolitionist to be the object of general detestation.

The despondency of anti-slavery men that followed their defeat in the struggle over the Missouri Compromise was not of long continuance. Already in 1820 the pen of Jeremiah Evarts, always ready and potent in a good cause, was busy in *The Panoplist*, showing that there was no reason for despair—that the condition of the negro population of America was still a legitimate subject of discussion, and the improvement of their condition still a legitimate object of effort on the part of patriotic and Christian men. The anti-slavery sermon of the younger Edwards, republished by Mr. Gurley, of the Colonization Society, was circulated both at the North and at the South. In the anti-slavery revival of this period, naturally enough, Andover Seminary largely shared. Of the six essays contained in the manuscript Transactions of its "Society of Inquiry Concerning Missions" of this time, not less than four relate to slavery and the colored people. The first of these, by R. Washburn, on the question, What is the duty of the Government, and the duty of Christians, with regard to slavery in the United States? begins thus:

"Perhaps there is not a more marked feature in the history of modern benevolent operations than the efforts made in favor of the unfortunate Africans. Forty years ago, there were few to weep over the wrongs and wretchedness of slavery; now thousands call the sons of Africa brethren, thousands are willing to devote their money and their efforts to redeem them from their long captivity, and thousands offer the daily prayer to Him who 'hath made of one blood all nations to dwell on the face of the earth,' that He would shorten the days of darkness and crime, and hasten that day of light and glory when oppressions shall cease, and a universal jubilee be proclaimed for all the enslaved of the human family."

The long report to that society, from the pen of Leonard Bacon, "On the Black Population of the United States," containing denunciations of American slavery as solemnly severe as could be expressed in language, was extensively circulated in New

England by the Andover students, and its severest anti-slavery passages were republished in Richmond. Every Fourth of July the most effective speakers among the Andover students went out into the neighboring towns to advocate the cause of the negro whether in slavery or in nominal freedom. The annual religious celebration of the Fourth by some associated churches of Boston, from the year 1823 onward, opened the famous pulpit of Park Street to the same subject, and there Louis Dwight, Leonard Bacon, John Todd and others in successive years spoke in no uncertain tones.

Naturally enough, the young men who went forth from this centre of anti slavery agitation did not lose their love of freedom in entering on the pastoral work. We follow the course of one of them, not as exceptional but as representative of the young clergy of the time; and we choose our example for two reasons, first, for our special opportunities of knowing his course, and secondly, because his name has been, and is to this day, systematically vilified as an example of the "universal apathy on the subject of slavery" prevailing in the community and especially in the Church, in the days before Garrison.

When Leonard Bacon, at the age of

twenty-three, took charge of the ancient church at New Haven, in 1825, one of the earliest incidents of his work was the organization of a club of young men, some of whose names were destined to become famous in the great conflict, under the name of "The Anti-Slavery Association." Out of the labors and studies of this club grew "The African Improvement Society of New Haven," in which he and his associates toiled with eminent success for the uplifting of the colored people of that city from their deplorable degradation.

In March, 1826, his friend Mr. Gurley, of the Colonization Society, wrote to him indignantly from Washington, of a speech of Mr. Everett's which he had just heard, apologizing for slavery. Said Mr. Gurley, " If he dares to publish these sentiments, which go to sustain a most iniquitous system, our friends at the North must not be silent." They were not silent. Mr. Bacon's Fourth of July sermon of that year, from the text, " Cry aloud ; spare not ; lift up thy voice like a trumpet, and show my people their transgressions," declared it to be " the duty of every citizen of the United States to promote by every means in his power the abolition of slavery "; and continued :

"Public opinion throughout the free States must hold a different course on the subject of slavery from that which it now holds. Instead of exhausting itself fruitlessly and worse than fruitlessly upon the *operation* of the system, it must be directed towards the *principle* on which the system rests. It must become such that on the one hand the man who indulges his malignity or his thoughtlessness in so exaggerating the evils attendant on the *operation* of the system as to implicate the body of the slaveholders in the charge of cruelty and tyranny shall feel himself rebuked and shamed by the nobler spirit that pervades his fellow-citizens; and such that on the other hand the man who dares to stand up in Congress and, presuming on the forbearance of those who sent him, attempts to purchase popularity by defending the *principle* of slavery, shall find himself greeted on his return to his constituents with one loud burst of indignation and reproof."

There was nothing startling in these views of the young preacher; they were the common opinions of the American Church at that time. He himself testified forty years later: "From the beginning of my official ministry, I spoke without reserve, from the pulpit and elsewhere, against slavery as a wrong and a curse, threatening disaster and ruin to the nation. Many years I did this without being blamed, except as I was blamed for not going far enough. Not a dog dared to wag his tongue at me for speaking against slavery."

It is an instructive fact already adverted to, that when the speech that so stirred the indignation of these two colonizationists reached Mr. Garrison in his editorial office, he found nothing in it to object to; he thought it a good speech, and printed it accordingly. He was at the time much concerned about the oppression of the Greeks. There does seem to have been "apathy" *somewhere*, in those days.

A favorite plan of the young men at Andover was the scheme of a college for the liberal education of colored youth. The scheme seems to have been first publicly announced by Mr. Bacon when, at the age of barely twenty-one, he urged it on the support of the Colonization Society at Washington in 1823. It was set forth more publicly yet in his "Plea for Africa" from Park Street pulpit in 1824, and at New Haven in 1825. It was much in his thoughts and in his letters. It met with a painful discouragement in the early death of Samuel Hooker Cowles, one of that circle of young Andover abolitionists, who was " willing to lend his hand to any measure which prudence and philanthropy might dictate," but whose cherished plan, as expressed in a biographical sketch in *The Christian Spectator* (1828, p. 4), was "the establishment of an African college, where youth were to be educated on a scale so liberal as to place them on a level with other men, and fit them for extensive usefulness to their brethren, either in this country or in the colonies." Not only in Andover was the plan taken up with eagerness. President Griffin, of Williams College, was its enthusiastic friend. Theodore Woolsey was earnest and wise in counsel about it; and his friend Ridgely wrote to Woolsey and Bacon:

"I am delighted with the idea of calling a general meeting at New York to deliberate about the practicability of establishing a *Negro University*. The necessities of Africa cry aloud for some such institution. Her children are starving for the bread of knowledge. They must have it. It is my opinion that twenty well educated and accomplished young negro *gentlemen* (I hope you are prepared for the unusual association of terms) would do more for that forlorn and outcast race than all that has been yet accomplished by their distinguished benefactors at Washington. It would go far to dignify the name."

Already, in the summer of 1825, the project had been talked over in the little Anti-Slavery Association at New Haven. It is needless to detail here the encouragements and the delays that it met with. At last, however, in the summer of 1829, the well-matured plan of the institution was submitted to a circle of leading citizens of New Haven, especially those connected with Yale College, and was cordially approved. A large conditional subscription towards it was made by a member of Mr. Bacon's congregation, and the scheme which for more than six years had been actively promoted by the friends of the negro race seemed in a fair way to be realized.

We have spoken at such length of the work done at New Haven as being an example of the humane and kindly work that was going on with increasing zeal and success throughout the North. There was not to be found in all the Free States a considerable city without its Clarkson Society or its African Improvement Society intent on similar labors. And the men and women who gladly gave their time, money and influence to promote this work were everywhere the earnest friends of that enterprise of African colonization, one great argument for which was its tendency to elevate the free colored people in America, and another great argument, its tendency to promote emancipation and the abolition of slavery.*

* *Christian Spectator*, II. 470-482, 521; IV. 318-331; V. 163-168.

At this juncture, in that series of Fourth of July discourses in which Mr. Bacon five years before had delivered his "Plea for Africa," Mr. Garrison makes his tardy entrance as an anti-slavery orator. The most notable characteristic of his discourse is the extravagance of his zeal for colonization. It was the one door of hope for the African race. It was to accomplish instantaneous wonders. But except for this and for his wild suggestion that the colored population of the country should be deported at the expense of the federal government, it does not appear that his speech differed materially from the half-dozen anti-slavery discourses that had preceded his in the same series. His impression that he was alone and peculiar in his sympathy for the blacks, "over whose sufferings scarcely an eye weeps, or a heart melts, or a tongue pleads either to God or man," was simply one of his constitutional eccentricities.

Coming forth in the summer of 1830 from his brief imprisonment in Baltimore jail, he made a progress through the northern cities in his character of martyr to the rights of the negro, making addresses to such meetings of the colored people as he was able to gather. Poor, ignorant, facile creatures, they were the ready victims of any demagogue who should cajole them with flatteries, or intoxicate them with silly expectations, or irritate their vindictive passions. These things Mr. Garrison was not ashamed to do, poisoning the minds of the colored people against the benefactors who had done so much for them, and were on the point of doing so much more, by representing that these were in a dark plot to keep them in ignorance and degradation.* The mischief that he wrought in thus defeating the fairest hopes then open before that injured people is not to be computed. The story of how, in unconscious coalition with the baser passions of the populace, he brought the noble enterprise of the African College to wreck is too long to tell at this time. He succeeded in identifying it, in the public mind, with his own pernicious teachings, and it was swept away by the shameful panic

---

* Address to the Free People of Color, by W. L. Garrison. Review of the same, *Christian Spectator*, IV., 311. The results of careful inquiry into the needs of these people, set before the charitable public to incite to sympathy and effort for their relief, were quoted to the blacks to show them that " those who have entered into this CONSPIRACY AGAINST HUMAN RIGHTS [the colonization enterprise] are unanimous in abusing their victims."—*Liberator*, I. 65. Also, II. 90.

Mr. Garrison's ferocious crusade against colonization was only an episode in his career, and need not be here detailed. The swarming fallacies and falsehoods in his "Thoughts on Colonization" (perhaps the most dishonest piece of polemic ever written) were exposed in the *Christian Spectator*, V. 145; but this did not hinder their being repeated over and over for the good of the cause, as they are still repeated for the falsification of history. See O. Johnson's "Garrison and His Times," 104, 109.

resolutions of a New Haven city meeting, but not without repeated solemn and indignant protests from Mr. Bacon, who lost in that ruin the hopes and patient labors of seven years.*

We must pass, rapidly, point by point, over the chief points on which Mr. Garrison fought against the anti-slavery cause, taking sides with its enemies.

As we have already seen, the stronghold of anti-slavery sentiment was in the Churches. In the progress of that pro-slavery reaction which began with Mr. Garrison's movement and moved parallel with it, growing with its growth and strengthening with its strength, those men did the noblest service to the cause of freedom who labored to hold the Churches to their principles. But they got no help from Mr. Garrison—only sneers and discouragements. His effort was just the opposite—to get all the anti-slavery men out of the Church, and turn the whole influence of that institution over to the enemy. For this purpose, he, and his confederates with his smiling encouragement, assailed it with

---

*See *The Religious Intelligencer* (New Haven), September and October, 1831. The editorial comments on this subject were well known to be from Mr. Bacon's pen. The story of this affair as told by Mr. Garrison's disciples makes the plan of an African College to have been an enterprise of "the Abolitionists" first broached two years before by good Mr. Jocelyn, and defeated with the guilty connivance and cowardice of Mr. Bacon. See "Garrison and His Times," 119-124. "Life of Garrison," I. 259.

unprintable vilifications, delighted if thereby they could draw a disorderly crowd to their meeting. As this went on, the best men among his adherents left him in disgust, and among those who remained were some who saw how suicidal was this course, and sought to arrest it, but were answered with defiance.* Was it strange that this

---

* At the annual meeting of the Massachusetts Anti-Slavery Society in 1842, Mr. Pierce, of Lexington, moved the following resolutions:
Resolved, As the sense of this meeting, that it is not by the use of opprobrious epithets and harsh and sweeping denunciations, but by speaking the truth in love, that abolitionists will best promote the cause of justice and truth.
Resolved, As the sense of this meeting, that in their writings, public discussions and private conversations, abolitionists should refrain from the indiscriminate censure and denunciation of whole classes and associations of persons, as the clergy and churches of various denominations, and all those who refuse to unite with them regarding such censure and denunciation, as unjust and highly impolitic.
Resolved, As the sense of this meeting, that the proposing, advocating or sustaining such resolutions as the following (which were discussed at a recent anti-slavery meeting), "that the religion of the United States of America is one vast system of atheism and idolatry, which in atrocity and vileness equals that of any system in the heathen countries of Asia or Africa or the islands of the Pacific Ocean"; "that the sectarian churches and ministry of this country are combinations of thieves, adulterers and pirates, and not the churches and ministers of Jesus Christ, and should be treated as brothels and banditti by all who would exculpate themselves from the guilt of slaveholding;" "that any man who goes to the polls and votes for a slave-owner or any other than an outspoken abolitionist, acts on the same principle with the Algerian buccaneer, and ought not to be recognized as an abolitionist"—manifests a spirit which, if at all consistent with the spirit of the Gospel, is not likely to gain friends to the anti-slavery enterprise, but bring upon it needless odium.

The quotations are a characteristic specimen of what used to pass for "eloquence" on Mr. Garrison's platforms.

Naturally, Mr. Pierce's resolutions were promptly laid upon the table; but when, two years after, Mr. Garrison moved that "the American Church was a synagogue of Satan," there was, of course, no hesitation about "resolving" it.

mad policy should have been so far successful as to inspire many good people in the Churches with a violent antipathy to the very name of anti-slavery or abolition?

One of the first conflicts in the struggle against the insolent aggressions of the slave power was to secure the recognition in Congress of the rights to which freedom was entitled under the Constitution and existing laws. The battle for the right of petition was fought out in the House of Representatives with splendid ability and heroic courage and endurance by John Quincy Adams. That good fight of his, single-handed against the crowd, is the finest chapter in our parliamentary history. The noble and venerable "old man eloquent," at the outset of the fight, was brutally stigmatized in the *Liberator* as "a dough-face."

The conflict was renewed again in the perilous days of 1851. That was a great day for liberty when Charles Sumner, elected to the Senate without the support of the Abolitionists and in spite of their efforts to defeat him, pronounced his masterly argument, "Freedom National: Slavery Sectional." This noble speech, which did so much towards bringing the nation back to its old bearings, and which struck the keynote of the march of the Republican party to its final success under the lead of Lincoln, was denounced by Mr. Garrison in a resolution as "false and absurd, and an outrage on common sense."* The little band of faithful men at the Capitol, the forlorn-hope of Freedom in her darkest hour—Seward, Sumner, Hale, Giddings, and the rest—were insulted, derided, discredited in the name of anti-slavery.

It was not in vain that these losing fights were fought out in the Houses of Congress. But the debate had to be held in a wider forum, and decided by the people. At the first Mr. Garrison had been impatient to persuade or drive men to the polls in an anti-slavery party. When, at last, the first beginnings of such action were taken (perhaps prematurely—there was a divided judgment among earnest men about that), they encountered Garrison's bitter mockery and denunciation. It was Resolved that a third political party is "fraught with unmitigated evil and mischief to the abolition enterprise." Those who sympathized with the effort—

---

* As usual in his extravagances, Mr. Garrison had begun by being preposterously extravagant on the other side of the question. In his Address to the Free People f Color, 1831, he had gravely advised his unfortunate clients that all the disabilities which they were suffering from unfriendly State laws could be swept away at one stroke by simply carrying a case up to the Supreme Court, from which august tribunal they might " walk abroad in majesty and strength, free as the air of heaven, sacred as the persons of kings."

such men as Birney, Hale, Leavitt, Whittier, Lewis Tappan—were made the targets of his contumely. Not only their persons, but in every important issue their cause, found in him an ill-wisher and an enemy. When freedom and slavery were in the grapple over the annexation of Texas, for all his stormy speeches about the wickedness of that measure, he lent no hand to prevent it, but hoped that "the slave power might become more and more severe," so as to bring to pass the horrors of that disunion which he was always coveting. He would dissuade anti-slavery voters from their duty as citizens, and deliver the question over to be decided by the enemies of freedom.

The war with Mexico was finished, and the question rose before the nation, what should be the destiny of the territories acquired from the neighbor republic. Freedom was never, in all the history of this conflict, so near a great, peaceful, and decisive victory as when the Wilmot Proviso, consecrating all that domain to free labor, was at issue. While good citizens were bending their energies to the struggle, the bird of ill omen kept croaking his discouragements. There was no hope; the nation must go on to disgrace and ruin; slavery must of necessity be triumphant; it is too late for reform; there is no remedy but revolution.*

The party of Free Soil kept growing in importance; but Mr. Phillips moved, and the Anti-Slavery Society voted (1843), that it was "a misdirection and waste of effort, and attempt at impossibilities." Like both the old parties, it was "essentially pro-slavery." The party adopted the bold and wise measure of planting an anti-slavery journal, *The National Era*, at the City of Washington, under Dr. Bailey, Amos A. Phelps, and John G. Whittier as editors. But slaveholders were assured that "if they knew the party and the editors, they would be relieved of all alarm." The sneers at Whittier might be justified on the ground of his having left the noisy camp of Mr. Garrison, and of the necessity of maintaining discipline by shooting deserters; but it could have been only the love of vituperation for its own sake that led to the denouncing of Longfellow for having in his noble lyric "The Building of the Ship," "prostituted his fine genius to eulogize the blood-stained American Union."†

The turning-point in the long fight with

---

* Mass. A. S. Report, 1847, p. 10.

† The quotations are from the Mass. A. S. Reports. Page after page these Reports are a continuous illustration of Mr. Garrison's constancy in getting upon the wrong side of every question affecting the cause of liberty, and abusing every one that was doing any useful work on the right side.

the slave power was reached when, after the perfidy of the Kansas-Nebraska Bill had been consummated, and at the moment of the almost despair of the friends of freedom, Eli Thayer, with heroic hopefulness and magnificent energy and ability, colonized Kansas with free settlers, and blocked the further extension of slavery. It is an almost incredible fact, and yet a fact, that Mr. Garrison and his little residuum of noisy followers did discourage and do what they could to defeat that noble, lawful and peaceful enterprise which gave checkmate to slavery and saved the continent for freedom. The story is authentically told by Mr. Thayer's own lively pen in "The Kansas Crusade."

It was in the flush of this triumph that the election of Lincoln was achieved in 1860. Both the platform and the candidate of the Republican party were in direct antagonism with every item of Mr. Garrison's distinctive principles.* And he was merely consistent with his principles in re-

---

*Mr. Lincoln repeatedly acknowledged his indebtedness for his definite convictions on the subject of slavery to the volume of Essays on Slavery by Leonard Bacon, which had fallen into his hands when he was a young man. The little book, now rare, is directed on the one hand against slavery, and on the other hand against that type of abolitionism represented by Mr. Garrison. It is from the preface to this book that Lincoln borrowed his much-quoted phrase, "If slavery is not wrong, then nothing is wrong."

fusing approval to the party, and consistent with his usages of speech in characterizing Abraham Lincoln as a "slave-hound." The helpers and counsellors of the great Emancipator, Chase, Seward, Sumner, Wilson, Wade, and the rest were subjected to like contumely.

Secession, long threatened, came at last, and found its friends and supporters, at the North, in Mr. Garrison and his little company. For many years the sagacious plan of Mr. Garrison had been identical with that of the Southern conspirators—though he expressed it differently—the founding of an independent, warlike, aggressive nation wholly devoted to slavery and occupying as its own the larger half of the domain of the Union, with as much more to the south and to the north as it might be able to seize and hold. It was part of his plan that the new nation should be started "peacefully," with every opportunity for strengthening itself in arms and alliances until it should be ready for offensive operations; and (if he could have his way about it) that the residuary northern nation should be organized on non-resistant principles, defending itself from its fierce neighbor only by the arms of love. A program more charming to the friends of slavery it is impossible to conceive. That they did not accept the treasonable invitation of abolitionist conventions to a "free correspondence with the disunionists of the South, in order to devise the most suitable way and means to secure the consummation so devoutly to be wished,"* could only have been because they knew how contemptibly insignificant was the faction from which the invitation proceeded. But if they had counted on what support the faction could give, they did not count in vain. "To think of whipping the South," said Mr. Garrison, "is utterly chimerical;" and he proposed to say to the slave States: "Depart in peace. Though you have laid piratical hands upon property not your own, we surrender it all in the spirit of magnanimity; and if nothing but the possession of the capital will appease you, take even that without a struggle." † On practical questions he was in cordial agreement with Davis and Toombs and Yancey and their confederates.

It is a most pleasant thing to record that the awful shock of war, when it came, did at last sober the chronic madness of the man. By his antecedents he was committed

---

* Resolution adopted at New York, December, 1859.
† *Liberator*, xxxi. 27.

"against all wars and all preparations for war; against every naval ship, every arsenal, every fortification; . . . against all appropriations for the defence of a nation by force and arms." * But now, to the astonishment of good citizens and the dismay of his old associates, he boldly turned his back upon himself, and rendered to the imperilled government and nation the best service in his power. There is nothing in all his career so honorable as his unfaithfulness, at this juncture, to his foolish so-called principles. According to these principles, the business of soldier was simple, unmitigated murder; but when his son starts for the war as officer in a colored regiment, he sends him off with his blessing for being true to his convictions, though regretting that these convictions are morally unsound. † War and slavery, in Mr. Garrison's view, were under like and equal condemnation. If affairs at that time had been on the old footing, and young Mr. Garrison had conscientiously believed, as many conscientious persons in the old times certainly did believe, that duty called him to be a faithful and humane master of slaves, it would have been a most pleasing and edifying spectacle to see the Reformer waving a parting salute to the young man as he

---
* "Life of Garrison," Iv. 231.   † "Life of Garrison," Iv. 81.

started for his plantation, saying, "I could have wished that you could see the matter as I do, but since you are faithful to your own convictions, God bless you, my boy." Unfortunately this degree of considerateness for the conscientious convictions of others, which Mr. Garrison so amiably manifested towards his own son, was not developed in his moral constitution early enough to save him from many painful and mischievous mistakes in his behavior towards other people's sons.

After all, Mr. Garrison did really, at the eleventh hour, come into the vineyard and take his place among those who had spent the heat of the day in practically useful and effective labors for the cause of human freedom; and who shall grudge him the remarkably large pennyworth of credit that he gets for it? It does, nevertheless, seem to be a public duty of considerable importance to correct some of the perversions of history that are attempted for his canonization. We have no ignoble discontent at hearing Aristides called The Just, no matter how frequently; but when it comes to a settled plan to keep calling Themistocles The Just, the case is different.

CONCERNING THE USE OF FAGOTS AT GENEVA

CONCERNING THE USE OF FAGOTS AT GENEVA.

FAGOT is one of that large class of common words that grow familiar to Americans in literature, but the meaning of which is not distinctly realized to the senses till we go abroad. To make sensible acquaintance with commonplace objects that one has known from childhood only by name is one of the delights of travel, as much as the seeing of famous places and pictures and buildings; and I believe that it is partly because they have so much more of this to do, that Americans are, beyond other nations, enthusiastic and delighted travellers. Doubtless one would go farther to see Melrose by moonlight than to see a teakettle simmering on a hob; but after all, to the diligent reader of his Scott and his Dickens, there are many like elements of pleasure in the two sights; and I will not too hastily decide whether I have more daily pleasure from the vast white pyramid of Mont Blanc, that looks me in the face through my parlor windows,* and "clear, placid Leman," down the slope beneath me, and the gray mass of towers of the old cathedral to my right, than comes to me from the magpies that chase each other chattering across the lawn, and the primroses and tiny daisies that blossom along our path under favor of this mild February, and the tufts of legendary mistletoe that hang in the bare poplar tree, and the hedge-rows, from which the gardener is now busy in gathering store of good material for next winter's fagots.

Which brings me back again to fagots, where we started. The fagot is not, as I used vaguely to imagine, a mere indefinite bundle of fire-wood. There is logic in its constitution, as there has sometimes been, in the severest sense, logic in its application. First, there shall be a handful or two of small twigs, such as the trimmings of the hedges furnish in generous abundance; then a handful of bigger brush; and finally, two, or at most three, stoutish sticks, to give solidity and respectability to the whole. These elements being brought together, then does the hedger cunningly lay about them a green and supple withe, and

---

* In revising this paper for its present use, the writer has not thought needful to wash out the "local color" that came into it by its being written at Geneva.

by some dexterous twist or double-hitch firmly bind them into one. With a few months' seasoning, the true and normal fagot becomes the ideally perfect commencement of a wood fire. A wisp of lighted paper, sometimes a mere match, is enough to start a combustion which matures, when properly sustained, into a solid mass of brands and coals. I often raise the question whether the enormous waste of small wood in all our forests, even those within easy reach of a market, might not be saved, and a fine opportunity of delightful employment given to workless city street-boys, if some one would only organize a phalanx of fagoteers for an expedition against the underbrush which is so often accounted a nuisance, but might so easily be converted into a blessing both to him that gives and him that takes.

It would astonish you to see in this woodless country, where coal is of easy access, how general is the dependence both for warmth and for cooking on wood fires; when, in New England, even farmers in little inland towns begin to feel that they cannot afford to burn wood on a hearth. If you were to ask me whence come the supplies on which the people here rely, I should refer you partly to the mountains, but rather to sundry lines of lopped and stumpy posts that intersect the landscape, bearing all over their wrinkled bark the scars of ancient wounds, and about their knobby heads, sometimes, chaplets of gay young sprouts, strangely in contrast with their aspect of venerable and bereaved old age. The Swiss woodman rarely ventures manfully to attack a tree at its trunk. He trims, he lops, he maims, he mutilates, and then he leaves the poor branchless, leafless stock to bring forth a new progeny for a renewed slaughter. Standing before one of these venerable boles, gnarled and hollowed out with age, yet making one more brave effort to put forth a growth of young branches, one is irresistibly reminded of some white-haired old "mammy" cherishing her last pickaninny of a grandchild, and telling the rueful story of two generations gone one by one to the auction-block. There is vast economy in this method, I am told. Managed with care, the mere shrubbery and ornamental trees on a gentleman's place can be made to yield his supply of fire-wood and hardly show any mark save that of judicious pruning. But oh! the ruthless cruelty of it as generally conducted! Hardly a tree in the canton of Geneva is suffered to grow in its natural shape; and the wide waste of reckless ruin around a charcoal pit on a Litchfield County hill-side is less sad than the double aisle of naked trunks of beech and oak that stand despairing in the hedge-rows between which I take my daily walk to town.

My fagot, as I find it waiting for me in the morning on my study hearth, sets me thinking on many things. I think of Roman lictors and their fasces; of " the good La Fontaine " and his fable teaching that union is strength; and as I strike a match, and the flame crackles through the twigs, and there is a smell as of a forest fire, and in a moment a fierce blaze shoots up the chimney, I think of Fox's " Book of Martyrs," and of Latimer, and Ridley, and others of whom the world was not worthy. For the fagot has been hallowed, like the cross, as the implement of death for religion's sake.

But most I am reminded of that October day, nearly three hundred and fifty years ago, when one of the first physicians of that time, and one of the greatest scholars of an age of great scholars, was brought out from the prison in which he had been shivering with cold and devoured by vermin, and led into the presence of the magistrates of Geneva to listen to this sentence:

"Having God and His Holy Scriptures before our eyes, and speaking in the name of the Father, and of the Son, and of the Holy Ghost, we do by this our final sentence, which we give herewith in writing, condemn thee, Michael Servetus, to be bound and led to the place called Champel, and there to be attached to a stake, and burned alive with thy book both in manuscript and in print, until thy body be reduced to ashes; and so shalt thou end thy days to give example to others who might commit the same crime."

The records do not inform us whether the school-boys at Geneva had a half-holiday the next morning, when the procession started from the prison at the top of the city hill for the place of execution at Champel. The principal figure in the procession, Servetus, though suffering from disease, and haggard, no doubt, from his imprisonment and from mental anguish, was a man in the strength of his age—he was forty-four years old, having been born in the same year with John Calvin. By his side walked Farel, the friend of Calvin, exhorting him to confess and renounce his heresies; but he only declared that he suffered unjustly, and prayed God to have mercy on his accusers. "Whereupon," says Farel, "I said to him immediately: 'What, what! when you have committed the worst of sins, you justify yourself! If you go on so, I will leave you to God's judgments; I won't go with you another step! I had meant to stand by you till your last breath.' After that, he did not say anything more of the sort. He prayed: O God, save my soul! O Jesus, Son of God eternal, have mercy on me!' But," says Farel, "we could not make him confess Christ as eternal Son of God."

They came, at last, to the place called Champel. Few visitors at Geneva see the spot. The people are not proud to show it. It is on a hill-side to the south of the town, commanding a fair view of the broad valley of the Rhone, and of the ancient city. The precise place is now covered by a house; but I have met old people who remembered when it was known as the *Champ du Bourreau*—Hangman's Lot— and who say that when they were boys there was a little pit in the midst of it that they used to point out to one another as the place where the stake was planted. Here the pitiful procession halted. With much persuasion the victim was induced to commend himself to the prayers of the people. And when he had kneeled down and prayed, he stepped upon the fagots that were heaped about the stake, and was bound to it by a chain about the waist; his book was hung at his side; a wreath of leaves dusted over with brimstone was placed on his head; there was one loud cry as the executioner brought up the lighted torch; but that was the end of it. Some say the fagots were green; but then old Mr. Gaberel's History may be right, that this was out of humanity, so that the suffocating smoke might put the sufferer more quickly out of misery.

"That was the end of it," we said. It seemed to be the end of it. But somehow this case of Servetus, in one shape or another, keeps coming into court over and over again from generation to generation. Generally, not to say always, it comes in the shape of a discussion of what sort of part it was that John Calvin had in the affair; and in this discussion a very needless amount of acrimony has been shown by some, who have seemed to think that the character of Calvin's theology, or of that great and splendid order of Christian churches of which he was the father, was somehow involved in the result. Let those on either side who have been discomposed by such a thought bear in mind that the discredit of whatever wrong Calvin may have done in this matter can fall only on those who accept and justify his course.

To defend Calvin for his course towards Servetus is no longer possible, in the light of the full array of evidence now accessible to every scholar. Something can be pleaded in mitigation. He was not, as is sometimes asserted, guilty of unfaithfulness to any principles of toleration of his own. Farel expressed his master's thought as well as his own, in one of the letters to Calvin in which he clamored for the death of the heretic. "Because the Pope condemns believers for the crime of heresy, because passionate judges inflict on the innocent the punishments which heretics deserve, it is absurd to conclude from this that the latter ought not to be put to death as a protection to the faithful. For my part, I have often declared myself ready to die, if I had taught anything contrary to sound doctrine, and that I should be worthy of the most dreadful punishment if I were to turn any from the true faith of Christ; and I cannot apply any different rule to other men." This point being established, the fatal conclusion followed; for it is impossible to dispute that Servetus was a heretic of an aggravated and dangerous type. He was no mere unbeliever, but a theologian intense in his convictions, with a plan for reconstructing theology, the church, and society, as set forth in his book of the "Restitutio Christianismi," or "Christianity Restored." And since he was a theologian of that period, it is needless to add that his manner of expressing his views was acrimonious and insulting to all antagonists, both Catholic and Protestant. Taking his career altogether, he does not appear to advantage in the figure of a martyr of free thought and fidelity to conviction, under which some would fain present him to us.

But admitting that according to the principles universally accepted in that age the execution of Servetus was justifiable, we are still far from any adequate vindication of the course pursued by Calvin in the affair. One of the latest contributions to the debate, and one of the fairest and most thorough, is to be found in Mr. Amédée Roget's *Histoire du Peuple de Genève*. Geneva is a very hive of busy antiquaries, among whom Mr. Roget is distinguished for his patient exactness. As a man of orthodox sympathies, he cannot be impeached of prejudice against Calvin. I think that his judgment in the case, delivered in view of important evidence that was not known to all his predecessors, is not likely to be reversed. Says Mr. Roget:

"The punishment of Servetus, considered in itself, leaves no very dark stigma on the reformer's character. But on moral principles that are the same in every age, Calvin stands condemned for having denounced Servetus to the Catholic Inquisition by the use of confidential papers, and for having delivered the unfortunate fugitive to the Geneva magistrates, when he was on his way to try his fortune in Italy. Granted that Calvin was in the line of his duty when he kept guard, in his way (which was the way of his age), for the security of the reformed churches. Had he any charge over the police of consciences in Catholic countries? Neither can we accept as natural, or compatible with a Christian spirit, the hard heart with which the reformer expresses himself to the end with regard to his rival, without so much as a moment's softening at the sight of the scaffold." *

* A still later volume contributed to the literature of this controversy is entitled "Servetus and Calvin; a Study of an Important Epoch in the Early History of the Reformation." By R. Willis, M.D., London. It is an interesting book; ambitious in style, and diligently prepared; but adds little to the work of previous authors, especially of Tollin, French pastor at Magdeburg, who has made Servetus his life-study. With the recent work of Mr. Roget, and with Pünjer's *De Michaelis Serveti Doctrina Commentatio*, Dr. Willis does not seem to have been acquainted. His volume is affected both by the *furor biographicus* and by the *odium theologicum*. It is not easy to make a first-class martyr to the truth, of a man who lied so easily under oath as Servetus, and who professed before the Inquisition his prompt readiness to renounce all his cherished convictions; and a cool judgment will decline to follow Dr. Willis in elevating him above Calvin and Luther as a theologian. Dr. Willis will be surprised to

Let us make every concession that the case admits. Doubtless Calvin was seriously anxious to prevent the propagation of destructive error. Probably the case of Servetus was complicated with political plots for the overthrow of Calvin and his work. Certainly the reformer made some motion to procure the commutation of the penalty to a less dreadful form of death. We will try to believe, even, what he tried to make himself believe, that there was no spark of human vindictiveness in all his efforts to compass the death of the man with whom he had for years been exchanging every sort of acrimonious insult. This is about all that can be said. But against

---

be accused of a theological spirit, having, doubtless, the prevailing impression that it is only Christian writers that are liable to this affection, and that disbelievers are necessarily safe from it. But his scornful ignorance of theological history and nomenclature betrays him into some strange blunders. The most remarkable of these is that of claiming for his hero the original invention of the "double sense of prophecy," which applies the words of the prophet primarily to a near event, and secondarily to a remoter one; and he illustrates this at much length from Servetus' edition of Pagnini's Bible, by instances which, he is sure, must have roused the orthodox rage of Calvin. If he had taken the pains to turn to Calvin's Commentaries, he would have found these identical expositions given to many of the same texts! As to the principle which strikes him as so bold a novelty in Servetus, he will find it as far back as Theodore of Mopsuestia, not to say as far back as the Apostolic Fathers. Theology may be a very unworthy study, out after all it is well to know something about it before undertaking to write on theological subjects. Dr. Willis's slip-up on such a matter as this tends to discredit that splendid air of omniscience with which he sweeps away all remaining doubt as (for instance) to the date of the prophets, and the authorship of the fourth gospel.

this we have before our eyes those fatal letters of Calvin's confidential friend, De Trie, which show the reformer in the act of furnishing the proofs to convict his antagonist before the cruel tribunal at Vienne, in France, and the sentence of that court predicated upon seventeen letters furnished by John Calvin, preacher at Geneva. We have that letter to Farel, of seven years before, in which, speaking of Servetus's offer to come on to Geneva, if Calvin wished, to discuss certain subjects with him, he says: "I shall make him no promises, for if he comes, and if I have any influence in the city, I shall see to it that he does not get out of it alive." We have Calvin's own avowal that the arrest of the furtive sojourner and the relentless prosecution that followed were of his instigation. We have the official record and Calvin's own version of the bitter, bitter wranglings between himself and the prisoner in the presence of the judges, and of his last interview with the condemned, on the eve of execution, in which he shows himself to the last the same fierce dogmatizer. And finally, we have his writing in self-vindication, when the dreadful scene was over, in which he taunts his dead adversary with not having formally restated, in the article of death, the doctrines for which he heroically perished, and seizes on his dying prayers as a proof that he had no sincerity in his opinions. It is in this same paper that he recites the appearance of Servetus, when his punishment was announced to him: "When the news was brought to him, he seemed at intervals like one stunned. Then he sighed so that the whole room resounded. Anon, he began to howl like a mad man. In short, he had no more composure than one possessed. Towards the end he got to crying so that he beat his breast incessantly, bellowing, in his Spanish fashion, *Misericordia! misericordia!*'" Through all these dismal documents, not one syllable of tenderness or human pity, unless it is in that letter to Farel, of the 20th of August, in which he says: "I hope he will be sentenced to death, but I wish that they may mitigate the horror of his punishment."

The prevailing motive that impelled the burning of Servetus was not less honorable than that which stirred in the bosoms of Caiaphas and the Sanhedrim on an occasion not in all respects unlike: "It is expedient that one man die for the people." Here was a golden opportunity for vindicating the reformed churches from that reproach of latitudinarianism that was thrown upon them by the Catholics. Thus wrote the pastors of Zurich when officially consulted on the matter by the Geneva magistrates: "We think it needful to show great rigor against him, and all the more as our churches are decried, in distant parts, as heretical, or as lending protection to heretics. Divine Providence now offers an opportunity to purge yourselves, and us at the same time, of an unjust accusation." It is a curious fact, repeatedly illustrated in ecclesiastical history, that persecuted heretics commonly seek to vindicate themselves from the charge of heresy by persecuting other heretics still more heretical. In the present case the fact has a double illustration; for among those who have given their strong approbation to the execution of Servetus is the most unexpected name of Dr. Jerome Bolsec, who had been hunted out of Geneva in peril of his life by the same John Calvin, for his unsoundness on predestination. He attempts to settle this account with his adversary by a "Life of Calvin" which is the reverse of a panegyric. But he protests therein: "I do not write these things out of any displeasure at the death of such a monstrous and stinking heretic as Servetus; I wish that all his like were exterminated and the church of our Lord well purged of such vermin."

This name of Bolsec brings to mind the story of his trial, the documents of which have lately been printed in full by another Geneva antiquary, Mr. Henry Fazy, and prove that the austere severity of Calvin in the case of Servetus was no solitary lapse under unwonted temptation, for his pursuit of Bolsec, if less fatal in its result, was not less truculent.

A century and a half ago, that malicious wit, Voltaire, who never knew how to do a generous thing without mixing it with a malignant stab at somebody, paraded the Servetus story in its worst light, by way of exhibiting Protestants as equally intolerant with Catholics. One of the most eminent of the Geneva pastors, Vernet, set himself to the task of refutation, and made application to the city council for access to the official documents, which at that time were under lock and key. He was surprised at the delays and discouragements which he encountered. The syndic Calandrini advised him that silence seemed wiser than anything that could be said. Vernet begged that at least three questions which he wished to put might be answered from the documents, and pressed his petition with some importunity. He received at last a letter from the syndic, of which he could not complain as wanting in explicitness. It ran on this wise: "The council considers it important that the criminal procedure against Servetus should not be made public, and does not wish it to be communicated to any person whatever, either in whole or in part. The conduct of Calvin and of the council was such that we wish it to be buried in profound oblivion. There is no defence for Calvin. Plead the state of your health in excuse for dropping a work which will either be damaging to religion, to the Reformation, and to the good fame of Geneva, or will be very unfaithful to the truth."

More than a century has gone by, and the archives of Geneva, and many a sorrowful document besides, are now accessible to every comer. But the advice of Syndic Calandrini to any one who would attempt the vindication, on this head, of the otherwise illustrious memory of Calvin, is as good advice to-day as it was then.

THE AMERICAN CHURCH AND THE
PRIMITIVE CHURCH

THE AMERICAN CHURCH,

AND THE

PRIMITIVE CHURCH.

THE two commonest conceptions of the church among American Christians may be characterized as the *Congregationalist* view, and the *Sectarian* view— both of them radically unscriptural and false.

1. The Congregationalist view holds that a church is a company of believers gathered out of the Christian community by voluntary association, and organized for worship and for other Christian duty. This view finds in every community of Christians as many churches as there are organized associations of this kind, and holds that every such congregation is an independent unit of sovereignty, owing duties of comity, courtesy, and fellowship to the rest, doubtless, but each in itself a complete church. Seeking its warrant in the Scriptures, it plants itself with immense strength on the undeniable, constant usage of the New Testament, which never speaks of "the church"

of a province, no matter how small the province may be, but always of "the churches." Little Achaia had no institution called "the church of Achaia"; but it had churches; and so with Galatia. The little patch of Asia Minor, which is the New Testament Asia, had certainly more than seven churches, but no "church of Asia." Corinth had its own church; and the harbor town of Corinth, Cenchreæ, nine miles distant, had its own church, too. The point seems inexpugnably taken against those who would hold that the church is a provincial organization stretching over a considerable region and embracing many towns.

But while holding this point so clearly, the adherents of this theory have resolutely blinked another point which is just as clear and constant, to wit: that the Scriptures, which never speak of *the church* of any province, equally refrain from speaking of *the churches* of a town. The Christians of a town multiply by thousands; they are disturbed by mutual alienations and serious variations in opinion, and strong personal attachments to different leaders; but they are always *one church* in that town; and if a division seems to impend, the apostle deprecates it with horror, saying, "I beseech you by the mercies of God, don't divide." All which is very unlike Congregationalism.

2. But it is still more unlike the alternative theory of *Sectarianism;* which holds not only that the Christian population of any town may properly be split up into different parties without common organization, but also that each one of these parties, entering into confederation with a like party in other communities, becomes thus a constituent part of a church—not of the town church where it exists, but of a sect of Christians extended over a nation or a continent. For this national party of Christians it calls by the name *Church;* though it is as far removed from anything known by that name in the New Testament as can well be imagined. In the dialect of the New Testament there are names distinctly applied to the sort of organization which we commonly call by the name of church. It is spoken of there as a $\sigma\chi\iota\sigma\mu\alpha$ or a $\alpha\H{\iota}\rho\epsilon\sigma\iota\varsigma$. We shall inevitably go astray in all our reasonings on this subject unless we bear in mind that this prevalent American use of the word *church* is one unknown to the Scriptures.

And it is well to remark, in passing, that this misnomer is not in the least justified by the fact that some one or other of these schisms or heresies is disposed to insist with somewhat obtrusive emphasis on the undeniable fact that the others are not churches. Of course they are not churches —any of them. A party of Christians is not the church, any more than a party of citizens is the state—any more than the part of anything is the whole of it.

3. And let me, in one more word, note a caution against one other misconception of the church, which I suspect to be prevalent —that the church of Christ is *the sum* of existing so-called churches, schisms, or (according to a favorite American euphemism) "denominations." According to the New Testament conception, the church is made up of the Christian people, not of Christian parties. It is "the communion of saints" —not a congregation of a selection of the saints. It is "the communion of saints," not the confederation of sects. The kingdom of Christ is the commonwealth of all humble and holy souls. His reign is within them.

Setting aside, thus, three untenable conceptions: (1) that a church is a club of Christians formed on some principle of selection out of a Christian community; (2) that a church is a sect of Christians constituted over a large region by the federation of such local clubs ; (3) that the church is the totality of sects ;—setting these aside, I propose this as the true conception, that the church of any place is the whole commonwealth of the Christian people of that place. There have been many "notes of the church" proposed by Christians of various parties,—form of government, pedigree of ordination, purity of doctrine, universality of extent,—always with a view to this: that the application of them shall prove each man's party to be the only church, and shall leave the other parties outside of it. But it is not difficult in reading the Acts and letters of the Apostles to recognize *this* as the one trait of the church as they understood it, that it was the fellowship of all the Christians.

Now while I acknowledge most painful defects in the organization of our modern, and especially our American Christianity, and while I look with earnest hope, not unmixed with anxiety, at the many movements toward a better state of things, I confess a lack of complete and unreserved sympathy with the lamentations that are often heard over the lost unity of the church, and with longings after a restoration of unity. For I cannot bring myself to account of the unity of Christ's church as of a thing that used to be, or a thing that ought to be attained in the future ; but as a thing that *is*—is *now*, as it was in the beginning and ever shall be. The religious affections of my heart fail to lay hold with any satisfaction on some fragment of a church which used to be one, and hopes to be one again. But I recognize and love, through all the ages and in every land, One Holy Catholic and Apostolic Church, the fellowship of all saints.

And that which I acknowledge and love as I look abroad over the great scope of the world and of history, I do not fail to find when I look about me in whatever place I find my work appointed—the one church, the commonwealth of believers. To the service of this, and not of any fraction of it, however pure in doctrine, however scriptural or historical in ritual, however correct in form of organization, however imposing by the magnificence of its extension—to the service of the whole fellowship of believers in the town in which I serve, I am devoted by the consecration that makes me the minister of Christ.

I am quite ready for that impatient interruption complaining that all this is quite out of time and place—that whatever may once have been true, and whatever may even now be true in some communities, in the American city of the nineteenth century the church is no longer one, but is divided. Divided? Yes, indeed. That which the Apostle Paul deprecated with earnest entreaty, adjuring the Christians of Corinth by the mercies of God that it should not be, has befallen us, that "there are divisions among us." Doubtless the Church of Christ in the American town is divided; but it is a divided unit—it is not many units. It is a divided church—it is not many churches, even though in our debased modern dialect we may combine to call it so. The one Church of Christ in the American town does not need to be created. It needs only to be *recognized*, and to be *manifested* to the world.

It needs to be *recognized* by its own members and ministers. It does not now offer itself to observation in any corporate form. It has no chief officer, the visible center of unity; no organized council or presbytery consulting for its united interest; no constitution or laws except the word of its Lord in the New Testament; but, men and brethren, you who believe in the Holy Ghost, do you doubt—can you doubt, so long as they who pass from death to life are known by this that they love the brethren,

—that in your own city, where you live and labor, the Church of Christ, one and indivisible, is a most solid reality?—the Church, with its cementing power of mutual love, so sadly hindered by ignorances and misconceptions, and by the miserable divisive spirit of sectarian allegiance; with its common zeal for its one Lord now wretchedly squandered in wasteful competitions; with its craving needs and duties, so often forgotten by its ministers in their exorbitant sense of duty to a narrow parish or congregation? Must you needs *see* this one Church of Christ before you can believe? Have you no sense of paramount loyalty and duty to the whole body of Christ's disciples, but only a little gush of sentiment, when you have given the devotion of your heart and the strength of your manhood to the supreme service of the party of Christians whose fortunes you are pushing with the spirit of a baseball game, as if the "emulations" which Paul condemns as works of the flesh were the very fruits of the Holy Spirit?

And just because I have small respect for that love for the one church which expends itself wholly in sentimental words, I bring the matter down to a most practical illustration:

From year to year, as the midsummer returns, is renewed the annual reproach of the American Church. In city after city, town after town, as the season of discomfort, danger, and sickness comes on, the Christian ministers, with the honorable exception of one great communion, and with certain individual exceptions beside, will, as a body, simultaneously forsake their charge, and leave the city deserted of its resident pastors. And each man speaking for himself will say, and say truly, that he leaves with the consent of his congregation, and that so far as his congregation is concerned this is the best time for him to take his needful rest. And no man will consider that each man is member of a college of clergy having charge of the common interests of the church of the whole town. If once the individual minister should learn to recognize in his own heart that the one church of the one Lord in his town was a most solemn reality, and that he was not merely the one pastor of his little fold of the flock, but also one of the company of the pastors of the whole flock, this annual scandal would at once begin to be abated.

This point simply by way of illustration of what might follow from the mere recognition in each man's heart and conscience of the doctrine of the Scriptures concerning the unity of believers, and the solid spiritual fact that they not only ought to be one, but are one.

And when I have said that the unity of the town church ought to be recognized by its ministers and members, I need hardly add that it ought to be *manifested* to the world. Being acknowledged in the individual mind and conscience, it certainly would be manifested, and that would be fulfilled which was spoken by the Lord from heaven, that the believers should be one, that the world might know that the Father had sent the Son. Whether that would come to pass which certainly did come to pass early in the primeval history of the church, that the town church should be represented by the town bishop at the head of the town clergy,—this might be—or might not be. But somehow or other the one church would find its voice, to which the world would love to listen.

Even now, he that hath ears to hear may hear what the Bride saith as well as what the Spirit saith. Every Christian town has its speaking monuments not only of the "competitive Christianity" which divides us, but of the common Christianity in which we unite. Every office of charity organization is a head-quarters of the one church ; and every individual charity from which is wholly eliminated the leaven of partizanship, so that, undertaken in the common love of Christ, and aiming at the common good of all for whom Christ died, it delights in putting glory on Christ himself and his whole church, is a work of the one church.

For the manifestation of the one church of their town, how good a work could be wrought by any two or three Christian men, who in a spirit wholly purified from partizanship should simply publish from year to year, with growing completeness, the Year-Book of the Church of Christ in that place, which should exhibit in love and holy pride and exultation the roster of its clergy and its meetings, and the works which each year are wrought there, through the divided congregations and the sharply competing sects, in the name of God's holy Child, Jesus ! Such a record, without one word of comment, would itself be a potent testimony to the general conscience, for Christ and his Church.

FIVE THEORIES OF THE CHURCH

FIVE THEORIES OF THE CHURCH.

THE author of the "Thirteen Historical Discourses on the First Church in New Haven"* vindicates the authority of that church, organized by mutual agreement in a meeting of the Christian people of the colony, by analogy with the civil government of the colony, organized in like manner, about the same time. After describing the "plantation-covenant," under which as a provisional government the colonists lived for fourteen months, the author records the meeting in Mr. Newman's barn, the framing of the church and of the state, the choosing of the "seven pillars," and finally the election and ordination of the church officers. He then proceeds as follows:—

"The question doubtless arises with some—Could such an ordination have any validity, or

---

* Thirteen Historical Discourses on the completion of Two Hundred Years from the beginning of the First Church in New Haven. By Leonard Bacon. New Haven, 1839.

confer on the pastor thus ordained any authority? Can men, by a voluntary compact, form themselves into a church? and can the church thus formed impart to its own officers the power of administering ordinances? If Davenport had not been previously ordained in England, would not his administration of ordinances have been sacrilege? Answer me another question: How could the meeting which convened in Mr. Newman's barn, originate a commonwealth? How could the commonwealth thus originated impart the divine authority and dignity of magistrates to officers of its own election? How could a few men coming together here in the wilderness, without commission from king or parliament, by a mere voluntary compact among themselves, give being to a state? How can the state thus instituted have power to make laws that shall bind the minority? What right had they to erect tribunals of justice? What right to wield the sword? What right to inflict punishment, even to death, upon offenders? Is not civil government a divine institution, as really as baptism and the Lord's supper? Is not the 'duly constituted' magistrate as truly the minister of God, as he who presides over the church, and labors in word and doctrine? Whence then came the authority with which that self-constituted state, meeting in Mr. Newman's barn, invested its elected magistrates? It came directly from God, the only fountain of authority. Just as directly from the same God, came the authority with which the equally self-constituted church, meeting in the same place, invested its elected pastor. Could the one give to its magistrates power to hang a murderer in the name of God—and could not the other give to its elders power to administer baptism."*

The argument thus popularly stated is sharply conclusive *ad hominem* against those who hold the popular statement as to the sanction of civil government. The American idea of the state implies the American idea of the church. The parity of reasoning betwixt the two is perfect.

But the analogy here drawn is good for much more than this. It has only to be cleared of expressions which point its immediate application to a particular class of gainsayers, to furnish a theorem by which, reasoning from sound principles in civil polity, we may discover fallacies, and establish the truth, in ecclesiastical polity. For several reasons, let us take the particular instance quoted above as the text of our whole discussion: first, because the argument will be clearer if stated in relation to a particular instance; secondly, because almost the only cases in which history distinctly discloses, side by side, the origin and earliest processes of civil and of ecclesiastical government, are this and like cases in early American history ; thirdly, because the passage quoted has actually been, in the mind

---

* Bacon's Historical Discourses, pp. 41, 42.

of the present writer, the germ out of which his argument has grown.

At the outset, let us guard against one source of misapprehension which will be more effectually obviated as the discussion proceeds. The church and commonwealth of New Haven Colony did not *originate* in the meeting in Mr. Newman's barn. They had existed at least fourteen months already. The " Two Hundred Years from the Beginning of the First Church in New Haven," which are commemorated in these discourses, date from the landing of the colonists, not from the mutual compact. And the civil state was coeval with the church. So that when it comes to strictness of speech, the question, Can men by voluntary compact form themselves into a church?—and the other question, Could the meeting in Mr. Newman's barn originate a commonwealth? are to be answered (so far as the present instance shows) in the negative. That meeting could not create what was already in existence.* What the meeting did was to *organize* both the church and the State. According to " Congregational usage" this is the same thing with originating them ;

---

* That this is the view accepted by the author of the "Discourses" is sufficiently implied both in the title-page and in the preface of the volume.

but according to the exact use of the English language it is something different.

Coming now to the question, What was the origin of the New Haven Colony Commonwealth and Church? and What were the source and channel of their authority, if any they had?—there is room for five different answers, according as the respondent holds one or another of five different theories of polity, civil and ecclesiastical. Let us name them:

    I. THE PAPAL THEORY.
    II. THE BOURBON THEORY.
    III. THE FORMAL THEORY.
    IV. THE JACOBIN THEORY.
    V. THE RATIONAL AND SCRIPTURAL THEORY.

I. THE PAPAL THEORY.

It is a "fundamental principle of the papal canon law, that the Roman pontiff is the sovereign lord of the whole world; and that all other rulers in church and state have so much power as he sees fit to allow them to have." Under this principle, the popes have claimed the power "not only of conferring benefices, but also of giving away empires, and likewise of divesting kings and princes of their crowns and authority." *

---

* Murdock's Mosheim, vol. II., p. 340.

The theory thus set forth is a very simple and intelligible one, and its application to the case in hand is nowise doubtful. The heathen territory of New England had been disposed of long before the Puritan migration by the gift of a pope to a Catholic prince,* and therefore whatever claim of jurisdiction should be set up within that territory by any body of colonists, whether in the name of a charter from a heretic power, or under color of a purchase from the barbarous tribes in possession, or under pretense of a so-called inherent right of self-government, must be simply an intrusion and a usurpation. It would be not only devoid of right in itself, but a violation of the divine right of the pope's grantee.

In like manner, any assumption of the functions of the church or ministry in this colony, otherwise than through the ways appointed by the head of the church, would be void and invalid, and therefore sacrilegious. Furthermore, it would be schismatic, as intruding a separate church authority within a territory and population already placed under the special spiritual jurisdiction of some bishop, or if not so placed, then remaining under the immediate pastoral care of the bishop of Rome.

---

* Bancroft's U. S., vol. i., p. 10.

Obviously, according to this theory, the first step for the colonists to take to secure a regular and valid government, in church and state, is to become reconciled to the Catholic Church.

II. THE BOURBON THEORY. This theory agrees with the first mentioned in declaring all lawful authority, civil and ecclesiastical, to be derived from God through a continuous succession of men. It differs from it in this : that whereas the former holds that there is but one line of this succession—the line of the popes—and that to all rightful secular and spiritual rulers, in any generation, their authority flows through the pope for the time being :—the present theory holds that the lines of succession are not one, but several : that from the original conferment, authority and "validity" descend along these lines, in secular matters through an hereditary succession, in spiritual matters through a tactual succession ; that the power of the sceptre and sword, or the power of the keys, as it is not derivable from the subjects thereof, so is not defeasible by them ; and that the question of title to authority, civil or ecclesiastical, is a simple question of pedigree.* According to

---

* See Macaulay's History of England. Chap. I.

this theory, the powers of the state centre in the sovereign. The king, not the pope, is "the fountain of honor." "*L'état, c'est moi,*" says the Bourbon; "*Ecclesia in Episcopo,*" responds the high-churchman.

In its two applications, to church and to state, the lines of argument by which this theory is sustained are very nearly equal and parallel. The state is a divine institution, and so is the church. The ministers of the one are divinely commissioned, and so of the other. There are difficulties objected in either case to any other external credentials of the divine commission than the credentials of succession from former ministers. Those whose claims to authority have been founded, exclusively or mainly, on hereditary or tactual relation to their predecessors, have been in a multitude of cases, and for many centuries almost universally, approved as lawful rulers and bishops. The two applications of the theory are analogous, not only by parity of reasoning, but by parity of unreasonableness: for in either case it is easier to show the several links of the succession than it is to demonstrate any law of cohesion by which they become a chain, or, the chain being completed, to hitch it fast to the original divine commission. It may fairly enough be admitted that the warrant for ecclesiastical power in apostolic succession, is as well accredited, on the whole, as the warrant of the hereditary divine right of kings.

Applying this theory to the case in hand, we find that the only right for the exercise of government which the settlers of New England generally possessed, was such as was conferred on them by charter from the king of England. Under such charter, if it was broad enough, all the functions of government might be exercised by the local magistrates in the name of the king. For lack of such authority, the legislative and judicial acts of the New Haven colonists were null and void. The only way in which regular and valid *independent* government could be set up in the little province of Quinipiac, would be for the colonists to import the regularly descended heir of some Lord's Anointed,—an Otho, or a grand duke Maximilian—and graft their wild olive with a slip of a Stuart or a Bourbon.

Likewise in spiritual matters, Davenport and Hooke might exercise such spiritual functions as their ordination to the priesthood by English bishops would authorize, but could acquire no new prerogative from any act of a self-constituted church. The way of maintaining the functions of the church from generation to generation, was to obtain other priests and deacons from the ordaining hands of the Bishop of London (whose modest diocese was understood by a mild fiction of law to include a large part of the Western hemisphere) ; or to secure, either from the lords spiritual of England, or from the cracked succession of the Scotch episcopate, the gift of a bishop with a pedigree sixteen hundred years long, whose should be all the rights of ecclesiastical sovereignty, to have and to hold, and to transmit to his assigns forever. Both these methods were practised successively by a few dissidents in the subsequent days of New Haven ; by virtue of which they became the real church of the colony, having the only " valid" and authorized ministry. For neglect of these, the body of Christian people in the commonwealth became schismatics and aliens from the church, and their so-called ministers became guilty (so we are assured) of the sin of Korah and of Dathan and Abiram.

III. The Formal Theory.—This theory appears under very different phases of development, and is held by very different parties of civil and ecclesiastical politicians. It is that the legitimacy, validity, or authority of a church or of a state are determined by the form of its structure. There are *jure-divino* monarchists, *jure-divino* republicans, and *jure-divino* democrats. So also, there are *jure-divino* tri-ordinary episcopalians, *jure-divino* presbyterians, and *jure-divino* congregationalists.

According to the first classes in these two lists, the state government in the Colony of New Haven was hopelessly vitiated because it did not constitute Mr. Eaton ruler during his life, and the head of an hereditary dynasty : the church polity was ruined, because the pastor, the teacher, and the ruling elder, instead of being in three ranks in a line of promotion, were all in one rank. And so, to the other classes, the colonial church and state must stand or fall, in respect to their divine sanction, according as they agree with or vary from a supposed "pattern showed to Moses in the mount." They came into being, as divine institutions, in the act of conforming themselves to the Scriptural model ; or if not so conformed, they never did come into existence at all.*

---

* For some severe animadversions against this test of churchhood—against "the whims of theoretic Biblists" and their "text-made churches," see Isaac Taylor's *Wesley and Methodism*, pp. 120 *sq*.

IV. THE JACOBIN THEORY.—This theory represents the body politic or ecclesiastic as originating out of the unorganized and unassociated materials of human society, by a "social compact" or "covenant," in which all the individuals agree, for the common advantage, to surrender to the new organization—the state, or the church—sundry of their individual rights and powers, to form the common stock of authority for the corporation. "The whole body is supposed, in the first place, to have unanimously consented to be bound by the resolutions of the majority; that majority, in the next place, to have fixed certain fundamental regulations; and then to have constituted, either in one person, or in an assembly, a standing legislature."*

According to this theory, the colonists of New Haven, from the time when they came out from under the authority of the ship's captain, at least until the close of their first day of fasting and prayer, when they formed their provisional "plantation covenant," were "in a state of nature." They were not a community, but only the individuals who might become a community whenever

---

* Paley's *Moral and Political Philosophy*, Book VI., chapter 3. See also Emmons's *Scriptural Platform of Church Government*.

they should agree to act in common. They were not society, but only the raw materials of society. There was neither a commonwealth nor a church among them, but only the possibility of these. By-and-by they concluded to have a state and a church, and so they got together in a barn and created them, appointing officers with divine authority for administering the functions of the two institutions—authority which up to that time had not existed in the colony. Before that, the execution of a malefactor would have been an act of murder,—either of private revenge or of mob-violence. Defensive hostilities against the Indians would have been simply the fighting of every man *proprio Marte,* except so far as individuals might have chosen to club together according to their preference for leaders. But any exercise of command on the part of him to whom the instincts of the people should turn as their natural military leader, or any attempt to coerce the shirks and the cowards into the common defence, would have been an act of tyranny and usurpation, there having been no unanimous mutual agreement of the colonists to concede their individual rights to this extent. And when, after experiencing the inconveniences of the " state of nature," the colonists began to frame their covenant, there was no right among them to compel into the arrangement any individual who preferred, at his own risk, to live among them but not of them, as a quiet and peaceable outlaw. The uncovenanted citizen might be derelict of a moral duty in thus standing aloof from the mutual engagements of the rest, but the powers arising out of these mutual agreements of ninety-nine of the population could not extend over the one-hundredth man who had declined to be a party to the compact.

Just so the Christian people of the colony were not a church, but only Christian individuals. The administration of baptism or the Lord's Supper, before the covenant, would have been, if not sacrilegious, at least a grave irregularity, and an infraction of Congregational order. The endeavor of them that were spiritual to restore by remonstrance and admonition a wandering brother, would have been the meddling of individuals in that which they had nothing to do with. The individual would not have been bound to submit to it; for "the obligation to submit arises from the bond of the covenant," * and he had never made

---

* See Emmons, who is beautifully explicit on this point. *Scr. Platform*, pp. 5, 7.

any such contract with his Christian neighbors. Any attempt to report the recusant in the weekly meeting of believers would have been both impertinent and futile; for the man never agreed to suffer any such use of his name, and the stated meeting of Christians is not a church, to "tell it to," because the members of it have not formed a social compact. The exclusion of an obstinate offender from the communion of saints is a sheer impossibility, because the saints do not have any communion. They are men of grace in a "state of nature." If, at length, the colonists hold a meeting in Mr. Newman's barn to arrange the terms of an association for mutual care, and contrive a covenant which should confer on the members and officers of the institution the divine right of enforcing a contract, it is optional with those who find themselves incommoded by too much "watch-care," whether they will enter into this covenant, or whether they will remain as lookers on, or whether they will form a little separate mutual covenant among themselves.

V. THE RATIONAL AND SCRIPTURAL THEORY.—This theory, as applied to the civil state, avoids encountering the hypothetical difficulties suggested in what we have called the Jacobin theory, by simply recognizing the facts of human nature. The questions whether an aggregation of human beings living together without any mutual interests or intercourse is a community or commonwealth;—whether "individuals are a civil society before they have formed themselves into one,"—whether "unconnected individuals, before they have laid themselves under a mutual engagement"* are the subjects of any common authority—are futile questions: as if one should ask whether a pile of quicksilver globules would constitute a pool of quicksilver before being flattened down; knowing that it is the nature of globules of quicksilver, not to stand in a pile like cannonballs, but to flow together upon contact. A battue of lions in an inclosure is not a herd of lions, no matter what discipline you may put them under, for the lion is not a gregarious animal. But a collection of horses or of sheep is a herd, or a flock, at once, without waiting to adjust the terms of an agreement, or to secure the valid investiture or ascertain the pedigree of the bellwether, because horses and sheep are gregarious. You do not have to constitute

---

* Emmons, Script. Platform, p. 4.

them a head,—they are a herd. Just so, if you gather human beings together in a separate population, you do not have to make society out of them. They *are* society, because man is a social animal. And wherever human society is, there are to be found, either potentially or in actual exercise, all the divine power and authority of the State.

And all the questions that are raised among the other conflicting theories of the State, as to the conditions, channel and credentials of divine authority residing in the rulers of the State, are shortly disposed of, according to the rational and Scriptural view, by recurring to that fundamental maxim, " The powers THAT BE are ordained of God." The government *de facto*, by virtue of its being *the power*, is charged by the Divine ruler with the responsibility of administering justice in the land, and is entitled to be respected and obeyed accordingly. This is the sole condition on which divine authority is conferred on the government of any country—that it *be* the government. With this agrees the maxim, in its only true meaning, that " all governments derive their just powers from the consent of the governed ;" since if this consent, whether voluntary or coerced, active or passive, is withdrawn, the power that was is no longer the power, and God does not ordain the impotencies. Without the actual possession of the power, no degree of *de jure* "validity" amounts to a divine commission;—not bulls from a pope, nor pedigrees running back to King David himself, nor any degree of ideal perfection in the structure of constitution, nor any certificates of a social compact in a mass-meeting. But, the power being present, not the absence of any or all of these conditions can discharge the *de facto* government of its responsibility, nor release the individual from his duty of subjection and obedience. Of course this statement is not to be interpreted to mean that all methods of acquiring civil power are right, nor that there is no preference among forms of government; neither is it to be applied to the exclusion of the duty of disobedience to laws requiring sin, or of the right of revolution. But properly interpreted and applied, this view of civil duty and authority is the settled result of Christian ethics.

Moreover, there always *is* an "existing power," residing in every community of men, latent if not active, which, whenever on any emergency it is called into exercise for the punishment of crime or the protection of innocence, carries with it the sanction of God.

Applying these principles to the case of the New Haven Colony, we find that before the "constituent assembly" in the barn, before the "plantation-covenant," the colony was already a state ;* and so any malefactor who should have presumed upon prevalent social theories to violate public or private rights or religious duties at that early period, would summarily have found it to be. His judgment would not a long time have lingered, nor his condemnation have slumbered, waiting for a social compact to confer the authority of a magistrate.

The divine right of government residing in the little commonwealth, might have

---

* "If a ship at sea should lose all its officers, or a shipwrecked crew be cast upon a desert island, this little community would then stand in the condition of a State. The whole would have the right to restrain and constrain each one for the freedom of all."—Hickok's *Moral Science*, p. 219.

It is necessary to guard against confusion between a *State* and a *State government*. The State government is the outgrowth or ordinance of the State. But, by a natural metonymy, the word *State* is often used to mean the government.

The students of "the judicious Hooker" will remember a passage in the "Ecclesiastical Polity" strikingly parallel to the above from President Hickok. It may seriously be doubted whether Hooker, if he had found himself in New England, would have felt that his principles allowed of the course of nonconformity and schism which has sometimes been pursued by those who call themselves his disciples and justify their practices by quoting his book.

come into exercise and manifestation, in various ways. Successive emergencies might have occasioned successive acts of authority, *nemine obstante*, which might have become precedents for others, and so a body of common law, and a sort of British Constitution, have grown up, without one act of deliberate legislation or foundation. The deference toward Eaton might, either explicitly or by the general acquiescence, have committed to him the supreme government of the colony, and at his death have transferred it to his son. Or the long-continued pressure of military exigencies might have habituated the people to martial law and settled their military leader into the seat of general authority. All these modes of the origin of governmental institutions in the colony are imaginable; and in any of them might have been inaugurated the power ordained of God. The method of sitting down consciously and deliberately to contrive the institutions under which the inherent authority of the state should express itself, is doubtless a nobler way; a way worthier of such matured and reflective minds as set up the pillars of the New Haven Colony—a way which has since become so exclusively the typical American way of organizing government that we are tempted to think it the only way; but it is not one whit more valid in conferring divine authority than the way practised in the insurrection on the slaver *Amistad*, when the tallest, nimblest and smartest negro in the lot elected himself captain and king, and exacted and received the obedience of the rest.

Now bringing the force of this extended analogy to bear on our main subject of the origin and authority of the church, we see at once the futility of those questions whether a neighborhood of "visible saints" "living members of Christ," while "separate and unconnected," constitute a church of Christ;* whether "a number of Christians merely living in the same city, town or parish,"† but having no common interests, no mutual affections, no stated meetings, and holding themselves aloof from mutual intercourse, are a church. The questions are predicated on an unsupposable hypothesis. That is not the way in which "visible saints" live. When they try to live so, their sanctity becomes invisible at once. They are no more, "visible saints," but visibly unsanctified. "By this we know that we have passed from death unto life, because we love the brethren." The prob-

---

* Ser. Platform, p. 3. * Idem. p. 5, and passim.

lem in theology that begins with supposing a neighborhood of Christians without mutual love and intercourse under the law of Christ, is as rational as a problem in magnetism which should be founded on the supposition of a collection of steel magnets having attraction toward the pole, but no attraction for each other. If, under the laws of human nature, human neighborhood implies human society, and human society implies the state; then *à fortiori*, under the laws of the regenerated nature, Christian neighborhood implies Christian society, and Christian society implies the church. The law of Christ concerning common and mutual Christian duties is already in force, and the authority of administering its earthly sanctions resides with the community of Christians.*

As touching the credentials of government in the church, it is hard to see where-

---

* It is amazing to see Dr. Emmons walking straight forward, with his eyes open, into the absurdity that the law of Christ begins to be binding on Christian disciples only when they have mutually agreed to be bound by it; and, by implication, that it is binding then only within the bodies that may be formed by "elective affinity," pp. 4, 5.

Quite in accordance with the Doctor's exegesis of Matthew xviii. 15–17, is the common construction of the same passage, which holds it to be a sin to report an offending brother in the lecture-room of the church until after the "first and second steps," but holds it permissible to advertise him "at sight" in the religious newspapers.

in the principle to be applied differs from
that which obtains respecting civil government. Under the latter, the individual is
required to "submit himself to the powers
that be." Under the former, he is required
to "obey them that have the rule over
him." In either case, the wide generality
of the command, interpreted by the inspired
absence of express instruction as to the
method of appointing and inducting valid
officers, points to a like conclusion :—that,
under the necessary and obvious limitations,
a *de facto* government, in church as in
state, is entitled to the allegiance of its subjects.

The illustration of this view by the instance of the New Haven Colony is so obvious that it is needful only to hint the main
points of it. The church which, according
to the uniform laws of the Christian life,
had crystallized out of the ship's company
during the voyage, having only such slight,
informal organization as the circumstances
of that temporary mode of life required,
was not dissolved when the colonists landed. It was the church authority subsisting
among them already, which was expressed
in the "plantation-covenant." When,
afterward, the town was "cast into several
private meetings wherein they that dwelt

most together gave their accounts one to another of God's gracious work upon them, and prayed together, and conferred to mutual edification," and thus "had knowledge, one of another," and of the fitness of individuals for their several places, in the foundation-work, or in the superstructure* —it is possible that they supposed they were preparing to *originate* the church ; but it is plain to the looker-on that the very act of "casting the town into meetings" was an act of the church. And the action of the "constituent assembly" in the barn was, like the adoption of our present national constitution, not the founding of a new church or state, but the peaceful revolution of one already in being. The Constitution does not make the state; the state makes the Constitution.

If, within the territory occupied by the colony, a knot of theorizers on politics had conspired to form a separate mutual compact for civil government among themselves, to use a different code of laws upon their members, and to secure a purer democracy or a legitimately descended ruler, the proper name for the act would have been *sedition*. Precisely so, when dissenters

---

* Bacon's Historical Discourses, p. 19.

from the colonial church *did*, for no grievance put upon their conscience, but simply in the prosecution of their church theories or prejudices, split themselves from the congregation, and refuse obedience to the existing government—" to them that had the rule"—and insist on importing for their special use a hierarch in the regular succession, the proper name for their act was *schism*.

But, on the other hand, let it be confessed that if the colonial Church had undertaken to exclude from its fellowship Christian disciples, for causes not demanding the censure of the Church nor discrediting the profession of a Christian faith—if they had reversed the gospel principle, and proceeded on the notion that it is better that ten weak disciples should be excluded than that one deceiver should be admitted—if thus they had created outside of their communion a party of Christians whose only opportunity of fellowship was in a separate organization ; then the sin of schism would have rested on the heads not of the few, but of the many. The Church itself would have become schismatic. But it is fair to say that this does not seem to have been the sin of the churches of the first nor of the second generation. The general prevalence of it in New England is comparatively modern.

OBJECTIONS TO THIS THEORY OF THE CHURCH.—The objections to be levied against what we have called the Rational and Scriptural Theory of the Church will exactly correspond with those which have been raised, to no effect, against the analogous theory of civil polity. They may be treated with great brevity.

Objection 1. The principle proposed, of the duty of deference to the *de facto* government of the Christian community, cannot be accompanied with any distinct and definite limitation, by which the occasional exceptions in favor of disobedience or revolution can be determined.

The answer to this is to be found, not only in the parallel doctrine and objection in civil polity, but " in almost every part of ethical science." So rarely is the exact boundary between right and wrong to be distinctly defined in a formula—so generally are the final questions on the application of moral rules left open for the decision of the individual conscience—that there is a *prima facie* presumption against any attempt to fix the course of right action on a point of morals by a formula of permanent and universal application.* The objection is a clear argument in our favor.

Objection 2. Under the doctrine here laid down, it will be impossible to justify the Puritan separations from the Church of England.

The first answer which we would make to this is that it is a small matter to answer it at all. The second, that a true judgment on those acts of separation must depend on the circumstances surrounding each act ; on the character of the parish church from which the separatists withdrew—whether it was Christian or unchristian ; on the nature of the grievances under which they labored, whether mere annoyances or actual burdens on the conscience ; on the probability of bringing the body of the Christian disciples in that community into union under a purer rule. The third answer is that if it does condemn the secession of dissenters from the Church of England, it thereby honors and confirms the judgment of our Puritan forefathers of the best and earliest age, almost all of whom, except the Pilgrims of Plymouth, abhorred the schism of the separatists with a holy horror. The

---

* See the ample illustration of this matter, in its political bearing, in Macaulay's History of England, Vol. II., pp 103-5, Harper's 12mo ed.

fourth answer will be conclusive in many minds,—that the doubt which it throws over the Puritan separations in England is more than compensated by the discredit which it puts upon many of the Baptist, Episcopalian, and Methodist schisms in New England.

Objection 3. This view discredits many of the local efforts for the propagation of Congregational institutions at the West and elsewhere, as schismatic.

Answer. Very likely.

Objection 4. This view brings in practical difficulty and confusion, by making it often a matter of doubt what is the Church of Christ in any community, and where its government resides.

Answer. This difficulty is not peculiar to the ecclesiastical application of the theory. It is of frequent occurrence in civil politics. Hardly ever is there a revolution or a considerable attempt at revolution, in which it does not become a very important and very perplexing question to some consciences— Which *are* " the powers that be?" It is a question not only for the passive and indifferent, but for the active leaders of revolution—first whether there is ground and need for revolution, and then whether the dissatisfaction of the people, the incapacity of the administration, and the combination of favoring circumstances have or have not charged them with *the power*, and with a trust for the redress of intolerable grievances, to the discharge of which they are ordained of God. Not to allude to questions which often arose to perplex honest consciences during our own civil war, the history of the mission of Dudley Mann to Hungary, in quest of a government to recognize, is one case in point. Another is the amusing story of Mr. John L. Stephens, whose Travel was never so full of Incidents as when, with a diplomatic commission in his pocket, he explored the various factions of a Spanish American republic, in search of the right government to which to present it.*

It cannot invalidate the principle which we have enunciated, that such difficulties are more frequent in ecclesiastical politics than in civil. In secular matters, the necessities of society are such that the rival pretensions of different claimants to the supreme government within the same territory become a nuisance so odious as not to be tolerable for an indefinitely protracted

---

* Incidents of Travel in Central America, Chiapas and Yucatan. By John L. Stephens.

period; and as for the settlement of these claims by allowing each claimant to govern its own partisans according to its own laws, the plan is so unnatural, so inimical to the peace of the community, that history has shown no disposition to repeat the solitary instance of it which is found in the present constitution of the Turkish empire, tempered though it is, in that instance, by the beneficent rigors of a supervising despotism.

But the union and communion of all the Christian disciples of any community, instead of being, like political union, a necessity, is only a duty. Consequently when once factions have established themselves in the Christian commonwealth, there is no necessary limit to their continuance from year to year, and from generation to generation. In the course of time the Christian mind becomes so wonted, and the Christian conscience so seared, to the wrong and evil of schism, that the doctrine of the perpetuity of schism is accepted as an integral part of the "evangelical scheme," and the sacred name of *the Church* loses its proper meaning, of the commonwealth of God's people, and becomes synonymous with its old opposite, a αἵρεσις or sect. The "problem of Christian union," which in the beginning no one ever thought of calling a problem, is held to be soluble only by diplomatic dealings between these churches (which are not churches), or else by setting up in the vacant place formerly held by the church, a new institution—a Young Men's Christian Association, or a Catholic Basis City Tract Society—that shall be the centre of Catholic affection and the means of the communion of saints.

In this state of a Christian neighborhood, doubtless the question, Where is the church? is a difficult one. One thing about it is plain, that it is not to be settled by applying worn-out tests, such as papal authority, apostolic succession, structural perfection, or democratic origin to any fragment of the schism, and determining that to be the Church. In some cases, it will appear that there is a Catholic church in the place, from which seditious spirits have torn themselves away in wanton schism. Sometimes, that the different churches, separate in name and form, are united in substance and spirit, that their several pastors, co-operating in every good word and work, are really a presbytery or college of ministers for the one Church of Christ in the town. Sometimes it will appear that the Catholic Tract Society has become a sort of church without ordinances, and that the president of the Society is actual bishop of the town. But more commonly the most that can be said is that the church in such a community is existing in a state of schism ; as, in the Rome of the twelfth and thirteenth centuries, the authority of the state might properly be described as dispersed among a number of families and factions. And the best that any one can do in such a case, is, while joining himself in special fellowship where he will lend himself least to the encouragement of faction, always to hold his supreme allegiance to be due to the interests and authority of the *whole* family that is named of Christ.

It is much in favor of any theory on such a subject as the one which we have in hand, that its chief difficulties lie in matters of application and detail. In these matters we would not speak with too much confidence. We may have wrought unsuccessfully in developing and applying the analogy which is the theme of our article. But we reach the close of the discussion with increased confidence that in the just treatment of this analogy lies the only hope of solving the problems of ecclesiastical polity.

THE RESTORATION OF THE PROTESTANT EPISCOPAL CHURCH TO CATHOLIC FELLOWSHIP

RESTORATION OF THE PROTESTANT EPISCOPAL CHURCH

TO CATHOLIC FELLOWSHIP.

THAT man will deserve well of the theological world who shall write, sympathetically but critically, the hitherto unwritten history of the projects and tentatives of Christian union. To be complete, such a history would have to go very far back toward the apostolic age ; for the effort after union is doubtless nearly coeval with the tendency to schism ; only, in the spiritual system, it is a sorrowful fact that down to our time the centripetal force has seemed to be overbalanced by the centrifugal. But the most accessible part of the story, the most instructive and practically useful to the church of the present day, is that part which begins with the first rendings of the Lutheran Reformation. The student who should enter upon this interesting task would be liable to some surprises at discovering how many and important are the facts and how considerable the literature pertaining to it. A better contribution to the cause of Christian union could hardly be made than by some such large review as we have suggested.

The motives that have incited to Christian union have been diverse and often mixed, and have taken a long range, from the highest downward. Sensitiveness for the honor of the church and high loyalty to its Head, love of the brethren, zeal for the more effective advancement of the kingdom of God—motives like these mingle or alternate throughout this curious history, with ambitions for a splendid and dominating hierarchy and Babel-plans of spiritual despotism, with aspirations after sectarian aggrandizement, and even with ugly animosities against one's fellow-Christians. Strange and abhorrent as the paradox may seem, it is a not infrequent thing in history to find plans of church union or federation springing from the spirit of schism, just as international alliances, offensive and defensive, are apt to be concluded when war is impending or intended. The holy sacrament of communion has been, in every age of church history, desecrated as the occasion of quarrel and mutual repulsion. From the beginning of them, the symbols of the Christian faith have been studiously contrived as *ecbols* for the "firing out" of certain Christians.* It admits of doubt whether any form of confession or any plan of church union has ever been proposed without a distinct recognition, either with regret or with glee, of the classes of Christians who were to be excluded by it. Plans of Christian union at their best and broadest have been plans for the union of *almost* all Christians, and generally plans purposely contrived for the exclusion of some Christians, or for admitting them under severe exactions.

It may justly be said of the basis of church union proposed by the bishops of the Protestant Episcopal Church in England and in the United States, that it is as respectable in its motive and its source, and as worthy in itself, as any of its predecessors. It is one of the happiest of many indications of the great advance of that denomination, especially in the United States, in every measurement of progress. In numbers, in wealth and influence, in intellectual and spiritual power, in true evangelistic zeal, in courage against public wrongs, and

---

* One of the earliest of these formulas was contrived by Bishop Cyprian with a phrase which, he flattered himself, would have the effect to keep the Novati ns out of the church—men who had incurred his just disapproval for their attempt to keep certain other Christians out. See Epist lxxvi, to Magnus.

pre-eminently in the difficult work of city parishes, it has made such advances in the last fifty years as hardly any other sect of the American Church has made. And it has shown itself able to bear this prosperity. Gaining in real self-respect, it has learned respect for others. Less and less do we hear of a certain snobbish pride in maintaining an elegant exclusiveness toward its neighbors, joined with impressive allusions to its distinguished relations in foreign parts. The most reluctant gainsayer is forced to recognize the evidences of a revival of religion, in the highest sense of that phrase, pervading the whole body. And among these evidences of revival none is more divinely attested than this, "that they love the brethren."

A most honorable and hopeful sign in the Episcopal Church of to-day is its "sacred discontent" with its peculiarly isolated position. It may be said, indeed, with some justice, that this isolation in which it has stood so long, cut off on all sides from formal communion with fellow-Christians, has been by its own fault; would it not be fair to recognize that its own virtue has had something to do with it? If it has cut itself quite loose from the church of the nineteenth century, has not this fact been incidental, or, rather, accidental, to a praiseworthy zeal for keeping up close relations with the church of the fourth century? If it has seemed sometimes to neglect the ordinary courtesies toward its immediate neighbors, is not something to be pardoned to the assiduity with which it has sought, however unsuccessfully, for recognition and acts of fellowship in the ends of the earth? Is it not proving itself a true vine, wholly a right seed, when, having so long reached its tendrils toward the East and found nothing offered for it to cling to (except the Old Catholics, if there are any of them left), it begins to turn with some sincere yearnings of heart to those toward whom it has hitherto cultivated a certain aloofness of attitude? It marks a dangerous stage in the process of freezing, when one loses the sensation of cold ; it is a symptom of the new and more vigorous life which is pulsating in the Protestant Episcopal organization, that the consciousness comes back to it of the chilliness of its practical separation from the Holy Catholic Church, the communion of saints. The dominating *motive and spirit* of the Protestant bishops in proposing " Articles of Church Unity" seems wholly right, honorable, and Christian.

This being so, there is no good reason for

being captious about the *manner* of it. If it seems to any to have, as enunciated at Chicago, the air of an invitation to the mountain to come to Mohammed, it is well to remember that at Lambeth it had much less of that appearance. If it shows itself a little diplomatic in scrupling some customary terms of courtesy, we are bound to consider the extent to which the body is embarrassed, in this matter, by its antecedents, and to honor the contrast which it now presents to the studiously supercilious and insolent style characteristic of its bad old days.

We come now to the *substance* of the proposed fourfold basis of unity, which is, in brief, the two Testaments, the two creeds, the two sacraments, and the Historic Episcopate.

On this, we remark at the outset, that in point of comprehensiveness it is far in advance of other projects of its class. On this account it cannot hope for the approval of those whose chief satisfaction with any plan of union or communion is measured by the good people that it keeps out. To such, the fact that this plan extends hospitable invitation to all heresies of later date than the fourth century is inadequately compensated by the fact that it sternly excludes

such modern saints as Buckminster and
Channing and Henry Ware and James
Martineau, and such as Joseph John Gurney and Elizabeth Fry. The exclusion is
a serious one; but, after all, it is doubtful
whether any project of Christian union has
been set forth which leaves so few of the
blessed saints in the outer darkness.

Aside from these exceptions, it will not
be denied that the various sects of American
Christians are as well agreed with each other
on the first three "articles of church
unity," the two Testaments, the two creeds
and the two sacraments, as the Protestant
Episcopalians are agreed among themselves.
Of course, the good bishops themselves do
not mean just what they say when they
speak of "the Nicene Creed as the sufficient
statement of the Christian faith." It is
doubtless sufficient and more than sufficient
for some purposes, and insufficient for some
other purposes: otherwise they would not
keep on printing the Thirty-nine Articles.
Nevertheless, as we have said, there would
be no difficulty about these three articles.
They are agreed upon in advance.

It appears, then, by this process of elimination, that there is only one condition lacking to enable the Protestant Episcopalians
to come into that fellowship with their fel-

low-Protestants which their souls long for.
This sole condition, in the language of the
bishops, is this : " The historic episcopate,
locally adapted in the methods of its administration to the varying needs of the nations
and peoples called of God into the unity of
His Church." Surely the partition walls
are worn thin, when this is all that remains
to separate. There is nothing hopeless, at
the present day, about this condition. The
situation is very different now from what it
was in those fierce old fighting days when
Independency and Presbyterianism were asserting each its *jus divinum*, and denouncing black Prelacy as a Man of Sin and an
infringement of the Second Commandment ;
and when the more or less judicious Hooker
in his Polity, and the mild Stillingfleet
in his emollient " Weapon-salve for the
Church's Wounds," were meekly pleading
for the right of bishops to exist. Nowhere
except in corners of Scotland and in some
of the transplanted Scotch sects is it easy
to imagine the old style of narrow anti-prelacy as prevailing at the present day. The
narrow exclusiveness in this dispute has
completely passed over to the other side.
There need be no despair of a general consent to the " Historic Episcopate." But it
would be needful to indicate more distinctly

what is meant by the phrase, and what sort of consent to it was called for.

What is meant by "the Historic Episcopate"? According to an old-fashioned theory still current among Roman Catholic scholars, the original form of the episcopate was the college of the twelve apostles, having a jurisdiction at large over all churches. This ideal is represented in our time by the powerful organization of the Methodist episcopate. Probably this is not the historic episcopate to which our consent or conformity is desired.

Beyond all question, the primitive episcopate, dating from the time when the form of church organization becomes distinctly a matter of history, was an *oppidan* episcopate, giving a bishop to every town, the president of the town clergy. This is the primitive type of the bishop of the sub-apostolic age. As we depart in time and distance from the early centres of evangelization, we find ourselves departing from this type of organization. It is to this model of episcopacy that it would be most reasonable, most hopeful, and most practically useful, to seek the consent of American Christians in general. That great scholar and representative Puritan, the late President Woolsey, remarked in conversation, "I would be in favor of an oppidan episcopacy." But, curiously enough, the persons most devoted at once to the historic episcopate and to the primitive Church are just those who would be most sorely discontented and recalcitrant at the acceptance of their " article of unity" on this basis so unmistakably historical and so undeniably primitive.

Coming down from the early ages and lands of the Church, we arrive, in the course of the iron ages of Christianity, at a gradual but revolutionary change in the office and function of bishop. His jurisdiction has widened out beyond the limits of the town and its outlying hamlets, and taken on the dimensions of a kingdom, including great and distant cities and teeming populations. There is a sense, no doubt, in which these novel functionaries, bearing the old name, may be said to belong to "the historic episcopate locally adapted," etc. But it is (to borrow a phrase from Oxford) a non-natural sense.

Another departure from the primitive and historic model has resulted, in the American Protestant Episcopal Church, from the exigency, so naïvely confessed in the preface of its Book of Common Prayer, of organizing itself as a sect over against other sects. This consists in the overslaughing of the proper authority of the bishop in his own diocese by the exorbitant powers of a periodical synod that stretches its jurisdiction over a continent, and assumes to control the bishop in his diocese in the detail of matters confessedly local and variable. Doubtless to have a sect organized for more or less friendly competition with other sects, this wide divergence from the ancient and catholic order may have seemed necessary. But if necessary, it is a necessary evil. This sectarian organization—the national consolidation of congregations of a certain way of thinking—is mightily helpful to a sectarian propaganda, but it is inevitably a copious source of local schisms. And yet it is much to be feared that this hurtful modern perversion of the ancient order is just what our good brethren at Chicago mean by " the historic episcopate locally adapted."

There is yet another form of " the episcopate adapted" which it is quite certain that there was no intention either at Lambeth or at Chicago to commend to the Christian public as a basis of union, but which, if only for completeness of statement, ought at least to be mentioned here ; we refer of course to that modification—quite in the line of the others which we have considered —which organizes the episcopate under a primatial see, and which has lately been urged upon us as a basis of union by a highly respected and venerated clergyman occupying a position of great dignity at the city of Rome. It might perhaps have been supposed that this proposal would fall in with the liberal ideas of "adaptation" entertained by the bishops at Lambeth, opening a way toward that larger fellowship to which they aspire. But from some remarks on the subject from the Archbishop of Canterbury, we conclude that in the matter of "adapting the historic episcopate" he draws the line just at that point. And a very happy circumstance it was for his Grace that he happened to take this view of the case, thereby avoiding all risk of the penalties of *praemunire*.

Evidently we can hope for no progress toward Christian union on this basis of "the historical episcopate adapted," until we come to a little more distinct understanding of what is meant by the phrase.

There is yet another point, of not less practical importance, that requires explanation. Of what sort, in the mind of the proposers, is to be *the application* of their condition of church unity? It seems to be intended to require assent or consent of some kind. Is it their idea to demand assent to their theory of church polity? But they have no theory. It would be impossible to frame in language a theory of church order on which they would be agreed among themselves. It must be safe for us to presume that they mean to exact nothing more in the way of assent than is required in their own ordinal; and that, according to our recollection, is the easiest possible. There is no difficulty just here. That man must be a hopeless sectarian indeed who cannot find a sense in which he can assent to "the historic episcopate," in the writings of such distinguished Anglican ecclesiastics as (for instance) Archbishop Whately and Bishop Lightfoot, and Deans Alford and Stanley, and Dr. Hatch.

But here comes a more embarrassing question: *To whom* is this conditional proffer of Christian fellowship tendered? Is it to individuals? Let us hope so, for in this case difficulties of the gravest sort are avoided, and a door of hope is opened to the Episcopal Church in America in the direction of a more catholic communion. (We say "in America," for it is only here that the question is a practical one. It is very pleasant to read the fraternal expressions of English bishops, but really they have about as little control over the matter as a convention of sextons would have. With them it is a matter for Parliament, and especially for that somewhat mixed body, the House of Commons, whose supremacy in such matters is an "adaptation of the historic episcopate" which we hope will not be too strenuously insisted on. The utterances of the American bishops are of more importance. They have not indeed authority over the matter, and there is room for painful doubt whether they could "carry their constituencies" in favor of measures to give practical effect to their sentiments. But they have at least votes and a share of power, and weighty and well-deserved influence.)

To return from this long parenthesis: if these overtures and conditions of fellowship are tendered to Christians and Christian ministers *as individuals*, the way is open at once for accepting them. We will undertake, if allowed a brief time for correspondence, to find and present to any one of the bishops who voted at Chicago, a company of godly and well-learned men, approved and honored as faithful ministers of the Gospel, and undeniably conformed to the four prescribed conditions, who will gladly accept the fellowship of the bishops in the same sincere and brotherly spirit in which it is proffered. What is the sort of hospitality to which they will find themselves welcomed? First, they will be put in quarantine for twelve months, during which they will be interdicted from all the duties and privileges of the Christian ministry. This being passed, they will be admissible to the narrowly circumscribed fellowship of the bishops and their clergy, on condition of severing themselves by permanent and irretrievable schism from the general communion of American churches and ministers. Still another condition besides the four named at Lambeth and Chicago they will find to be rigorously exacted, to wit, that they shall conduct the offices of public worship always in conformity to an ancient Act of the English Parliament (1 Edw. vi.), which seems to be looked upon as universally and divinely obligatory upon American Christians; and that they shall refuse to do the duty of preachers of the Gospel to congregations worshipping by a different rite.

If, writing without opportunity of reconsulting the canons that cover the case, we have made any important mistake as to the course prescribed, we shall gladly accept corrections. If, on the other hand, our statement is substantially correct, in what sort of light does it leave the Lambeth-Chi-

cago overtures for Church unity? We are
confident that those overtures were offered
with a genuine sentimental sincerity; but
practically what better are they than a
plausible and not very ingenuous bid for
proselytes?

The answer to all these difficulties must
needs be that the four "Lambeth articles"
(to use an old phrase in its new application)
are not intended to apply to individuals,
but are only offered as a basis of negotiation
with other sects or "religious bodies."
The statement confronts us with difficulties
still more formidable. The former difficulties could be removed by the amendment of
a few arbitrary canons. We now meet with
difficulties that are deeper seated.

Waiving the very great but not desperate
difficulties of opening and conducting negotiations and then of securing the ratification
of them on the part of both the high contracting parties—supposing these, by the
grace of God, brought to a successful issue,
and terms of union or confederation agreed
on with the leading "religious bodies" on
the basis of the historic episcopate—what
then? Why, then, doubtless, with the necessary modifications of its canons (which can
just as well be modified without such diplomacy as with it), the Protestant Episcopal

Church would be let out from its seclusion—a most happy and desirable event. But would the common historic episcopate thus conferred have so much as a tendency to promote the unity of the church? Would it not tend rather to the sanctioning, the confirming, and the exasperating of schism? Let us look soberly into these questions.

Two plans have been suggested for the uniting of the church on the basis of the episcopate. One is that the "religious bodies" should be consolidated under one government in which all should be represented, and in which each should have full liberty within the easy limits of "the quadrilateral." The other is, that without attempting governmental consolidation, there should be communicated to representatives of each of the "religious bodies" that which constitutes the essential historicity of the episcopate. If there is a *tertium quid* to this alternative we are not informed of it. The first course would give us a huge corporation, the constituent members of which would be, not "faithful men," but organized and embattled sects trained and drilled through ages of schism to the practice of competition and emulation and other "works of the flesh." The second course would give us just what we have now—this scandal of scrambling, hustling, and competing sects, holding nevertheless quite sincerely certain terms of fraternal fellowship with each other—with only this difference, that thenceforth the Protestant Episcopalians, perhaps the most shamelessly scrambling and hustling "religious body" of the lot, would feel itself at liberty, without sacrifice of its dignity and consistency, to fraternize along with the rest.

Is it possible that any have been dreaming that the historic episcopate would change the elements of human nature? Happily we are not left without experimental proofs on this point, and these nigh at hand. Our brethren of "the Roman obedience" have an historic episcopate—very historic indeed, as well as in a high degree "locally adapted"—but it seems to have had no effect whatever in bringing them into exceptionally fraternal relations with their historically episcopal neighbors; in fact, the effect of it, as far as visible, seems exactly the reverse. A case quite in point is that of the Moravian Church—name never to be mentioned without love and veneration—which was in occupation here with its bishops forty years before the Episcopalians, and whose historic episcopacy is certified by the highest authority in the English Church, an Act of

Parliament ; but what token of favor or fellowship has it ever had from the Protestant Episcopal Church? So far as we are aware, only this : that the amiable Bishop Stevens was kind enough to reordain a Moravian presbyter in order to give him "a more ample ordination ;" and this is an amplification that any of us might have had on the same terms. There is still another case, which can hardly have occurred to the minds of the bishops at Chicago when they were yearning for union with their Protestant brethren on the basis of the two Testaments, the two Creeds, the two Sacraments, and the Historic Episcopate. Close at hand was the very object of their hearts' desire. And yet we do not remember to have read, in any account of their meeting, of their having sent a special message to the Right Reverend Bishop Cheney and his presbyters, and of his being received by them with embraces and effusive expressions of fraternal delight. It may have happened, but we have seen no record of it. We are not questioning in the slightest the personal respect and affection with which this eminent and excellent partner of theirs in the historic episcopate is regarded by them in their hearts. But so far as strictly ecclesiastical fellowship is concerned, we have seen no evidence that the Reformed Episcopal Church, for all its Testaments, Creeds, Sacraments, and Episcopate, comes any nearer to satisfying the longings of the bishops for union with somebody, somewhere, than the "religious bodies" that are less distinctly conformed to the four conditions. In fact, all indications are directly to the contrary. By reason of the closeness of its filial likeness, the Reformed Episcopal Church is a less eligible object of fellowship than we who are afar off. In the language of the poet Gilbert, it is "too, too all-but." We cannot resist the conviction that the bishops at Chicago, good, honest brethren speaking out of the sincerity of their hearts, nevertheless do not know their own minds in this matter. If there is any instruction in their own history and in Church history generally, the more nearly any one of the other "religious bodies" is approximated to them, the more unwilling they would be to have fraternal relations with it.

Let us prognosticate a little. Suppose negotiations on the "quadrilateral" basis to have been successfully concluded by which the two leading bodies of Presbyterians, North and South (about 7000 ministers and 1,000,-000 communicants), and of Methodists, North and South (about 20,000 ministers

and 3,500,000 communicants), should be
united with the Protestant Episcopal
Church (about 4000 ministers and 500,000
communicants) ; the resultant either will
be a governmental consolidation or it will
not be. If the former, will any imagination venture to forecast the course of debate
and business in the first General Synod or
Council of the new Church, when (for instance) the question arises whether the Reverend Dr. Briggs is taken in or left outside
by the first of the four conditions of union ?
If the latter, in what respect is the intercommunion among the sects confederating
on the quadrilateral basis, of any greater
efficacy for good than the intercommunion
already existing among what are called the
evangelical denominations, except that the
new arrangement will take in the Episcopalians? The existing intercommunion, on
the basis of common faith and hope and
genuine though imperfect mutual love and
respect, does not suffice to save the country,
and especially the West, from wasteful and
scandalous competitions. Is there the ghost
of a reason for thinking that by adding to
this basis the common claim to a historic
episcopate the practical mischiefs of schism
would be one whit diminished ?

It is not even probable that the desired

union would diminish the number of sects. The King of Prussia had two Protestant sects in his dominion; he was resolved to have only one; when he had got through with his work he found that he had three. The Roman missionaries in the East mourned over the division of Eastern Christians; they labored strenuously to draw all together on a basis not wholly unlike the "quadrilateral;" they succeeded so well that at last they had nearly twice as many sects as there were to begin with, with the Latin sect to boot. Is there any practical lesson in these bits of history?

If we may imagine the proposed unification to go on so near to achievement as that the number of sects in our American Christendom should be reduced to two, we should then be farther from our end than before, by as much as that the intensity and acrimony of sectarian animosity would then be raised to its highest power.

We cannot regard the present critical position of the Protestant Episcopal communion in relation to church union, amiable and praiseworthy as it is, without something of anxiety lest the general interests of the One Church suffer detriment. It would be a serious loss to the true cause of Christian unity if, through the impatience of

Episcopalians with an irksome isolation, the Church of America should lose the benefit of their unwelcome but salutary protest against the sin of schism. Almost all the other Protestant sects have lapsed into the habit of regarding schism as the right and normal order of the church. We all recognize the common strain of talk at Evangelical Alliance meetings and like occasions, how that the separate sects (we beg pardon— denominations) are ordered by Divine wisdom, and the more of them the better ; how that the prismatic colors blend into the white light ; how that the horse, the foot, the artillery, and the sharpshooters combine to make up the sacramental host ; how competition is the life of business and emulation one of the works of the Spirit ; but nevertheless how beautiful it is, like the ointment upon the head of Aaron, for brethren to dwell together in unity now and then for an hour at a Tract Society meeting or an Evangelical Alliance ! In the midst of this general defection from the foundation principles of the church, it has been a wholesome thing for us to be forced to listen to the persistent, uncompromising protest against all this cant, from one of the minor sects. The fidelity with which this protest has been reiterated in men's reluctant ears may

well be called heroic. Against affectionate
entreaties, against angry denunciations of
bigotry, and narrowness, and Pharisaism, the
little party of High Church Episcopalians,
itself the merest sect of a sect, has answered
all invitations from its "sister churches"
with stout denials: "you are not sister
churches, you are only sects; there is only
one Church, and we are it; sects have no
right to exist. You ought, all of you, to
come into the Church, the ark of safety, instead of lingering without, having no hope
except in the uncovenanted mercies; especially you who are assuming to act as ministers of these religious bodies, you are involved in the guilt of Korah, and Dathan,
and Abiram; if you wish our fellowship in
the ministry, you must be admitted to it in
the only way—through ordination by the
historic episcopate, of which we hold the
monopoly." Not only against denunciation and entreaty has this protest asserted
itself, but (what is harder to bear) against
the frequent smile and the occasional laugh.
For it is impossible to deny that the situation has sometimes been extremely funny.
But it has been bravely persisted in nevertheless—all the more honor to the conscientious illogical brethren who so stuck to
their principles without seeing the humor-

ous aspects or the moral consequences of them.

It is a matter of serious anxiety to observe, with the vigorous growth of "Broad" principles, a weakening of this sturdy and long-sustained protest, and a disposition (as in this "quadrilateral" manifesto) to fall into the easy, popular course of compromise with sectarianism. The hope of church unity does not lie that way. Negotiation among sects as such can lead to nothing higher than a union among sects as such, and a union of sects as such never can be the Church. A confederation of sects wears no seamless robe; its proper drapery is a crazy-quilt.

We are reluctant to let go the long-cherished hope that some time a logical mind would be raised up in the High Church party among the Episcopalians who should show his brethren what their position implies. This party, which has long been completely dominant in that "religious body," has never really taken itself seriously. Otherwise it could not have helped seeing that by "High" principles it was bound in conscience to the broadest of broad policies. It has claimed for its communion, "this is not a sect, or a denomination, this is the Holy Catholic Church for America.

This is the one channel of sacramental grace, outside of which are no covenanted mercies. This alone can confer that authority without which the assumption of the duties of the Christian ministry is an awful sacrilege. This is the one ark of safety." But instead of feeling the momentous responsibility of such a trust, and flinging wide the happy gates of Gospel grace, and offering welcome to all believers, it has planted itself across the gang-plank of the ark and forbidden entrance to all but those who conformed to a confessedly arbitrary system of rules of etiquette. Its communion claims to be the Church Catholic; but is "run" in the spirit of the narrowest and most sectarian of sects. Liberal enough where narrowness might have been excusable, solemnly strict at points at which it was bound by its confessed principles to be freehanded and comprehensive, it would seem to have taken for its government an ancient and most catholic maxim, "locally adapted" to its own temper and convenience: *in necessariis libertas; in non-necessariis unitas.*

If that should come to pass which seems indicated by the signs of the times, and the High Church party in the Episcopal Church, having had everything its own way for so long, should be superseded in its dominant position by the young and able and rapidly growing Broad Church party, we should feel that while something had been gained by the change, a valuable opportunity had been missed and wasted, and a door of hope for the peace and unity of the Church of America had been shut fast. We venture to repeat here language that was written just twenty-one years ago on the occasion of Dr. Döllinger's forgotten little Christian Union convention at Bonn :

> The hopeful way out of the practical difficulties of schism, especially in America, is not that of diplomacy among doctors of divinity of various sects, but that which begins at the other end, with seeking a way of reconciling local sectarian divisions in little villages. I believe that the Episcopal Church in America, if it only knew its mission, has some grand advantages for this work. If it could rid itself of sundry canons that bind it hand and foot, abate a little of that high-and mighty tone which is so apt to make people smile, and apply to such a ministry of reconciliation one half of the energy now expended in fomenting local schisms at home and in begging for recognition and Christian union at the ends of the earth, it might do a great thing for itself, and a greater thing for American Christianity, and make all other Christian communions grateful to it in spite of themselves.

O Jerusalem, if thou hadst known !

We commend to the bishops who spoke at Lambeth and at Chicago, and to the "religious bodies" who may be attracted by their proposals, the study of the system, and methods, and traditions of the Roman Catholic Church. There are greater and better things to be studied in that venerable institution than those matters of pomp and pageant and millinery that engage the attention of petty minds. There is its sense of duty and responsibility and its scale of missionary endeavor, not wholly out of proportion to the magnificence of its pretensions. There is its elasticity in adapting itself "to the varying needs of the nations and peoples" of which we see a signal and admirable illustration before us in the United States at this very time. There is its distinction, clearly recognized, if not always justly drawn, between the variable things and the constant things in Christianity. And withal (a matter which the popular impressions completely misconceive) there is its faculty, of which Anglicanism has shown a characteristic insular and John-Bullish incapacity, of comprehending within the harmony of a single system diverse races, languages, rites, disciplines, theologies, and temperaments. It does not insist that the Eastern nations shall learn the Latin language or adopt the Roman rite. It permits among them a married clergy, and holds itself free at its discretion to introduce the same liberty among the Western nations. It admits (though it tries to discourage them) traditional variations of ritual "use" in individual dioceses. But especially it admits diverse and sharply controversial schools of doctrinal theology, maintaining each its separate missions and its separate congregations, and cultivating each its favorite specialties in religious work, inciting each other with a perilous intensity of emulation and even envy, and, strangest of all, keeping up each its own discipline, independent of the authority of the episcopate. In short, that which in Protestantism would be a schism, tearing itself from the Church with ruthless rending, and organizing itself into a sect of aggravated and acrimonious temper, under the masterly statesmanship of the Roman polity is geared into its complex machinery and becomes an Order in the Church.* Is there in all this

---

* We would like to be informed by any who are skilled in the literature of the subject, whether the striking analogy between the sects in the fellowship of Protestantism, and the Orders in the unity of the Roman Church, has ever been brought out in its instructive details. Protestantism, as well as the Catholic Church, has its Benedictines, its Dominicans, its Jesuits, and its Capuchins, to say nothing of other mendi-

no instruction and warning to be laid to
heart by an institution that is in danger of

cant orders. It may justly be claimed, on the one hand, that
under the visible divisions of Protestantism there is an un-
derlying unity ; as on the other hand it would have to be con-
ceded that under the formal union of the Orders under the
obedience of the Holy See, there have sometimes raged the
fiercest passions of sectarian hatred. The story of the mutual
animosities of the different Orders of missionaries in China
could not easily be paralleled from the history of the Protestant sects. But all things considered, it is wonderful and admirable how little there is, or, at least, how little there is
known, of violent discord or mischievous competition in so
complicated and risky an organization as the organization of
the regular Orders inside the lines of the secular hierarchy,
but independent of its authority.

Every one will recall the strong antitheses of Macaulay in
contrasting the comprehensiveness of the Roman Church
with the martinet rigidity of the English. "At Rome, the
Countess of Huntingdon would have a place in the Calendar as
St. Selina, and Mrs. Fry would be foundress and first Superior
of the Blessed Order of Sisters of the Gaols. Place Ignatius
Loyola at Oxford. He is certain to become the head of a formidable secession. Place John Wesley at Rome. He is certain to be the first General of a new Society devoted to the
interests and honor of the Church." We are aware that the
author quoted is not a favorite in the American Episcopal
Church ; but for all that, this passage from the review of
Ranke contains " wholesome doctrine" for it " and suited to
these times."

Of course the likeness between the Orders of the Roman
Church and the sects of Protestantism does not extend to
all points. The division between the Orders goes no further
down than the clergy ; the layman is neither Dominican nor
Franciscan, but simply Catholic. Among Protestants the par-
titions cut down to the lowest strata of the people. In like
manner in the other direction, at Rome, the division extends
upward as far as the General of the Order, but is limited by
the paramount authority of the Vicar of Christ ; among Protestants the division extends on and up, limited only by the
paramount authority of Christ himself, when this authority is
able to get a hearing for itself.

combining lofty pretensions to the exclusive authority and communion of the Catholic Church with the narrowness and light-minded irresponsibility of a Protestant sect? The Lambeth and Chicago manifesto seems to betoken that the leaders of Anglicanism have begun to get a glimpse of their false position. Unhappily it seems also to indicate that they are ready to fall into a new position no less false than the old.

www.ingramcontent.com/pod-product-compliance
Lightning Source LLC
Chambersburg PA
CBHW022052230426
43672CB00008B/1150